THE DO-RE-MI OF SINGING

THE ULTIMATE BEGINNER TO INTERMEDIATE SINGING GUIDE

AVENTURAS DE VIAJE

WARNINGS AND DISCLAIMERS

CONTENTS

THANKS FOR YOUR PURCHASE

Did you know you can get FREE chapters of any SF Nonfiction Book you want?

https://offers.SFNonfictionBooks.com/Free-Chapters

You will also be among the first to know of FREE review copies, discount offers, bonus content, and more.

Go to:

https://offers.SFNonfictionBooks.com/Free-Chapters

Thanks again for your support.

INTRODUCTION

Welcome to this wonderful guide. I hope that your journey here will be one of enjoyment and growth. I used my resources and knowledge to create this wonderful guide to help you on your journey towards bettering your singing skills. I also want this guide to be helpful to both beginners and those that have been part of the singing world for longer, and I think the inclusion of all the practice exercises and tools that I will be discussing will allow you to learn new techniques no matter what your skill level.

This guide has been split into two different sections. The first section will be the beginner section that consists of four chapters. The second section will be the intermediate section that will also consist of five chapters.

The beginner section will cover all the basics from finding your own sound all the way to finding the best genre for you as well as the best tools and practices for a beginner, or even a seasoned artist that wants to get into a new genre. The intermediate section will cover more in-depth practices and tools to help you better your skills and practical ways of keeping up with trends and techniques.

By splitting the guide into these two sections, I was able to split the work and skill levels far better than having one encompassing guide. This allowed me the best possible way to create the most appropriate methods for practice and the best tools to help you no matter your skill or knowledge level.

I will also be including a small glossary at the end of this guide. Please refer to this section if anything is unclear. This section will help guide you through the intermediate section where industry specific wording will be used. This is especially important for beginners or those who have just started their research section for singing.

I do cover some sensitive topics in the final chapter of the intermediate section. The chapter contains a section surrounding anxiety and how to best treat it. Always seek professional help before engaging in recreational activities or taking any sort of medicine for something like anxiety.

I hope that this guide will teach you the fundamentals that every artist needs and wants as well as help guide you through the best practice tools for your trade. This guide can be used no matter what your skill level and I have used the best tips and tools to make it as accessible as possible.

PART I

BEFORE YOU BEGIN

Here, I will be covering all the basic information you need to consider before starting the long journey to becoming a vocal artist. While I encourage everyone to try every hobby out once, it is important to remember that some people are naturally gifted for some activities whilst others need to work harder and longer hours to achieve the same level of comfortability. I will start off with basic criteria that while not every person needs, it is often found when looking at successful artists around the globe.

These criteria are:

- Singing in a choir, whether it is a religious or youth group. Being a part of a musical group will allow you the gauging capacity to know how hard you have to work as a solo artist, or as a group.
- Vocal coaches are an amazing investment and if at first it seems expensive or time consuming, it is well worth the time and money later on.
- Practice, at home especially, but also whenever you have free time. Practice scales and make a song selection that is perfect for your voice type, and practice it over and over.
- Choral camps are an amazing place to better your skills and learn tips and tricks from other singers.

While these criteria are not definitive and you don't need to have all of them ticked off, they are great starting points for everyone. While some of these might not seem doable for adults, there are wonderful platforms all over that allow you to learn from the comfort of your own home, providing you the time and place to advance at your own pace.

It is important to be sure that this is the path you want to follow, especially if you want to become a professional artist. The entertainment industry is definitely not for the faint of heart, and even the best of the best seem to struggle. So making sure that you are dedi-cated, disciplined and able to perform your best in front of large crowds will only allow you even more success than before. These three things are the most important to remember when choosing a professional singing career.

1. **Dedication:** You will need to dedicate a lot of your free time towards practicing skills you have yet to learn and mastering ones that you only know the basics of.
2. **Discipline:** Giving up your free time is the least of your worries when it comes to becoming a professional singer; you will have to dedicate a lot of time and energy into becoming a good artist.
3. **People Skills:** Being able to deal with large crowds of people and taking the time out to spend time with fans and supporters will allow you to better engage as a performer, and being able to deal with fans and the large amount of stress surrounding public appearances is a definite skill you should either work on if you are a little shy.

While there are other skills you need to be able to become a successful vocal artist ,there are quite a few tools you will need as well. Whilst these tools are not entirely necessary, I do suggest using them to make the training and exercises easier for yourself.

Various different artists and coaches all have different approaches to what tools you would need and how to use those specific tools, so my best suggestion would be to try everything out at once and see what works for you. There are a lot of things that will influence how easily you will adapt to different singing styles.

TOOLS OF THE TRADE

There are various online resources and guides that can help you learn how to sing, but it is important to be realistic and honest with yourself. Sit down and consider what you truly want to do in the music industry. There are so many moving parts in the music industry, and if you are uncertain that is perfectly fine as well, but I seriously do suggest sitting down and weighing the pros and cons of the different paths that you might want to pursue. It is important to remember that each path in the following list is vastly different. Each path will have its own earning potential, longevity, benefits and even limitations. Considering the pros and cons for each of these paths will allow you to better understand yourself and the musical career you want to have.

The music industry, of course, covers more paths than just the following list, but I opted for these paths since they are mostly vocal orientated. The list of following paths are open to any and everyone:

- Recording Artist
- Singer and/or Song-writer
- Musical Theater
- Folk and/or Indie Singer
- Band Member (backing vocals or lead singer)
- Soloist
- Jingle writer and/or singer

Each of these pathways will open up different doors for you and they each require different types of attention and commitment, so choosing and laying out a path of what you want to do within the music industry.

It is important to remember that getting into singing might just be a hobby, but it can also turn into something much more than a hobby or relaxing activity, and the fact that you are reading this guide means that you are far more interested in making this something more than just a hobby. Be sure that you are ready to be able to put in hours upon hours of hard work, sweat, and tears.

One of the most important things to also consider when starting your singing journey is your knowledge surrounding musical notes and being able to read music notation, this will however be discussed later in this chapter. This will help you along your journey of figuring out what genre you will enjoy the most, and what type of musical path you want to follow. It is important to embrace a musical lifestyle and environment to help you better and easier learn the skills you need. If you are still in high school or studying anything other than music theory some of these ideas might not apply to you, but if you are able to consider doing some of the following it would greatly help your education towards singing better.

Consider some of the following when you know that you are dedicated to the music pathway you have chosen.

- Moving to bigger cities, especially since some cities are known for music creation and offer a larger variety of opportunities to help you grow. While you don't need to move, and you can use a social media to create a platform where you have access to more opportunities
- Get educated. Getting any sort of musical education will always help you, no matter what you are learning. It is important to remember that the more knowledge you have about a certain topic, the easier it will be to learn and get better at something. Consider taking an online class surrounding music theory, or performance, or even going on to YouTube and watching a few educational videos surrounding performance.
- Do different things. While this is very broad, I would suggest looking at different places and activities you can use to better your performance skills. Activities such as talent shows, music festivals, and even charity events or fundraisers.

- Promote yourself. This is going to be hard work, but the best way to get out there is to create various social media platforms to create a presence where people can access your talent even when you are sleeping or busy with a fundraiser.

While these are not the only things you can do to jumpstart your singing, it will allow you to create a better social appearance to help you improve your skill and craft. In the next section I will cover the basic tools you will need to be able to better your singing and music knowledge.

There are various physical tools that you can use to help you on your musical journey. It is important to remember that knowing the basics around music and music notation will help your entire journey. This will help both beginners and those who are more intermediate within the music industry.

There are various tools that you can use to better your knowledge and skill set. The basic tools that most beginner or hobbyist singers are the following:

- Keyboards, whether it is an actual keyboard or an online or software version one.
- Pitch pipes, this will allow you to better understand the range and pitch of a new song you are learning.
- Metronomes are used to help you keep a steady pace for a song.
- Recorders are wonderful, especially when you are starting out, to help you learn new songs and their range and pitch.
- Private instructors are amazing to have but they are not always the easiest or most cost efficient to invest into when you are starting out, but I would suggest considering this option.

BASIC MUSIC NOTATION

As mentioned before music notation and being able to read music notation is one of the most important things an aspiring singer can do. Being able to read sheet music will help you become a better singer. Here I will discuss the basics of music notation and sheet music reading.

When looking at sheet music it will look similar to the image below.

The horizontal lines are called the staff. There are 5 lines in the staff that are vertically spaced.

The clefs on the left side will indicate the key signature that each section is supposed to be sung or played in. Modern music only uses four different clef signatures. Those are called the Treble Clef, Bass Clef, Alto Clef and Tenor Clef. Each of these dictate a different range of singing.

It is important to remember that each clef starts on a different note when the music starts. The two most common clefs that are used are the treble clef, more commonly known as the G clef, and the bass clef, more commonly known as the F clef. In the image above the first clef is a G clef, while the second is an F clef.

The vertical lines that are found on the sheet music are called the measures. Time measures are used to create divisions in the music. These time signatures also dictate the amount of beats in a section. Whenever you find a thicker line, it will show the beginning or ending of a music piece. You will also often find small numbers at the top of the measures, helping you to read the music in an easier way.

In the following chapters I will cover the basics of voice health, pitch range, genre selection and some basic exercises.

VOICE HEALTH

Voice health is important to any singer, and immediately when you think of voice health you consider things like vocal exercises and making sure not to force yourself to create certain sounds. Here, I will cover the best ways to keep your voice healthy and strong for any performance, as well as include basic voice exercises.

Taking care of your voice is important, especially if you want to make sure that you can create the best possible sound no matter the genre you choose. While exercising your vocal cords are important, it is also important to remember that overall physical health will help you perform better.

To be able to perform at your best, it is important to take care of your overall physical and mental health. There are various things that you as a learning musician can do to keep your body in tip top shape and your overall health on a good level. While each musician does different things to relax and keep themselves happy and keep their mental health on a good level, it is up to you to decide how you want to do that. Before going into the best exercises and methods of keeping your voice healthy and happy I will cover some ways to help keep *yourself* happy and healthy.

One of the best ways to keep healthy is by following a good and balanced diet, including things like blueberries, which are packed with antioxidants that help oxygen intake, and fish, which is packed with Omega 3 that helps voice health, into your diet will help your body recuperate and allow you to build a healthy lifestyle. There are various foods that can help your voice and the smoothness it needs when you are practicing.

Always be aware of the amount of sleep you are getting and if you are getting quality sleep. While sleeping enough is important, it is also important that the sleep you get is quality sleep where you don't constantly wake up and roll around. There are various methods of making sure that you get enough sleep. Some people might suggest taking some medicinal remedies whilst others suggest leaving all technology out of your space for at least an hour before going to bed. There are various ways to relax before heading to bed, try some of the following activities to help you relax and calm down before heading to sleep, allowing you to get optimal rest:

- Yoga or meditation will allow you to focus on what's truly important and relax before bed.
- Taking a warm bath or shower before heading to bed will also allow you to calm down and let your muscles relax after a long day.
- Drinking some warm milk, or chamomile tea will also help you relax, letting your mind at ease, allowing you better capability to sleep as much as you need to.

Focusing on your health is something very important and making sure that you are healthy will help your learning process become much smoother and a far easier process. While taking care of your voice it is important to do the correct vocal warm ups to help your learning process be as easy as possible. Doing vocal warm ups before strenuous voice exercise and even before just singing a few bars will help you in the long run, especially for newer singers who might try out a genre that's far more taxing on the vocal cords than you'd think.

Keeping Your Voice Healthy

Keeping your voice healthy is extremely important and activities such as smoking, vocal abuse like screaming can drastically have an effect on how your voice functions and the capabilities you have. When you do not take care of your vocal cords and voice you may end up damaging your voice far more than you think. Keeping your voice happy and healthy will allow you to sing whatever genre you want.

There are so many things that you can do to keep your voice healthy, and each singer has their own ritual and routine for keeping their voice healthy. I am going to share some basic tips on how to let your voice live its best life.

1. Warm up and cool down

The reason behind this has been discussed earlier but this is one of the most important things to do.

2. Hydration

Hydration and warm herbal teas are amazing ways to keep your voice happy. While hydrating during exercises and warm ups is very important, it is also important to keep hydrated throughout the day. Keep in mind that small sips of liquid won't always lubricate enough so make sure to try and stay as hydrated as you can by having enough liquid with you.

3. Humidifiers

Humidifiers are amazing pieces of equipment that will help the hydration process for your voice. Dry air is extremely bad for your voice so having a humidifier will help your overall voice and respiratory health as well as keep your voice from drying out too much.

4. Vocal Naps

Like working out, it is important to have rest days to allow your voice to rest, especially when you are working on a big project or trying out a more taxing genre. Like with going to the gym, when your muscles are tired you are more likely to hurt those exact muscles, similar to this you can hurt your voice if you overexert it during a practice or performance.

A common thing that most people don't realize is that whispering is bad for your voice, especially when you are about to record a new track or have an audition, be sure to rest your voice from any sort of movement or strain, even talking.

5. *Harmful Substances*

Harmful substances can be classified as anything like smoking and vaping, and yes even secondhand smoke can cause issues for you in the long run. While these are not the only harmful substances that can be inhaled, they are the most dangerous and have the most permanent effects of all the substances. These inhalation particles dry out your vocal cords.

Alcohol is not as severely damaging to your vocal cords, but it can cause inflammation for your vocal cords and dry them out, making it difficult to sing certain notes and tones, and forcing yourself to do so after a night of drinking and/or smoking can cause permanent damage to your vocal cords.

If you are currently a smoker, even if it is just casually, I would suggest giving up the habit and trying your best to stay away from anything else that is as damaging. To counter these effects, try your best to keep your voice hydrated and lubricated during warm ups, singing lessons, recordings and even during cool down and resting periods.

6. *Throat Singing*

When you consider all of the above information you would assume that you are merely singing from your vocal cords but you are not. One of the most important things to remember when it comes to vocal health is to make sure that you are singing from your diaphragm, chest and pharynx. This is called singing from your core. This is extremely important as it will allow you to relax your vocal cords, taking the strain off of them and letting the sound resonate from your chest.

This is not an easy process and will take some time to get used to, this is normal and with practice and perseverance you will be able to do this in no time. Make sure that you do warm up exercises that include this, allowing you to practice while also slowly building up to the more strenuous parts of the activity. Having a vocal coach to help you with this will also help the process along rather quickly and in a safe manner as they will guide you on what is best for you and your voice.

7. *Pain*

One of the most important things to remember when singing is to not over exert yourself. While I understand that hours of work and finally being able to hit that elusive note is amazing and you feel the adrenaline and excitement rush through your veins, it is important to remember never to push yourself beyond your capabilities.

Forcing yourself to sing past a certain point is extremely bad for you, and forcing yourself to sing through pain is even riskier. When you are in pain it can cause serious damage to your vocal cords, resulting in either surgery or being unable to sing again. If your throat hurts, take a break, rest as much as you can and hydrate even more. Do not engage in drinking or smoking or going out when there is cold weather; try to stay warm and comfortable to keep from hurting yourself even more.

8. *Diet*

As mentioned before, your diet has an impact on how your vocal cords react and change during practice and performances. It is important to know what the different types of food offer your body and vocal cords in order to give you the best possible results.

The type of diet that works for most artists and helps them achieve the goals they want usually consists of lean proteins, whole grains and plenty of fruits and vegetables. Whilst it is not always easy to constantly consume these types of food, it is important to have food like this before an audition or big rehearsal. These food types will give you increased energy and stamina.

I would suggest staying away from most dairy products before rehearsals and auditions, but even during practice sessions, as dairy can thicken mucus and make it difficult for you to reach the notes you want, in turn putting strain on your voice.

While a healthy diet is important for a healthy singing voice, you need to consider that eating a full meal before a rehearsal or audition is not as smart as you may think. I would suggest eating at least an hour before rehearsals and about 90 minutes before a performance, as your body needs time to digest and eating anything heavy might leave you feeling bloated and sick. A full stomach can and will press against your diaphragm, making it more difficult to breathe and will naturally keep you from getting better range.

As mentioned before, hydration is extremely important, and while drinking water and herbal teas will help you I would suggest being careful when it comes to the amount of caffeine that you consume, as caffeine will dehydrate you slowly. Be sure to use herbal teas that contain peppermint and licorice, as this will help you with any inflammation you might have.

9. Improvement

There are amazing ways to improve your singing and skills. You can use as many skills, videos, and online resources as you want but the best way to get better is to get a vocal coach that can help you. Your voice, like every single other voice, is extremely unique and the best way to get your voice better than others is to find someone who can help your unique voice reach better heights.

While I don't think that online guides and videos are bad, I do think that they can only offer you so much assistance, so having a coach or trainer help you get better and more skilled with your voice. This will also help you expand your vocal range, give you the capacity to smoothen the bridge you have and allow you to not overexert yourself or your voice.

10. Signs of Strained Vocal Cords

One of the last things you need to take notice of is when your voice might be going under strain, and oftentimes that is quite difficult to see, especially if you are new to singing and you are uncertain about what is needed and what is not. It is especially common when people try new genres and are uncertain of certain breathing techniques.

There are various symptoms that can indicate that you are straining your voice and you need to take time to rest. Some of the following things are indicators that you have overexerted your voice:

- Tightness or pinching at the back of your throat
- Hoarseness
- Scratchiness
- Missing notes while singing

These symptoms are clear indications that you need to rest your vocal cords and take some much needed time away from singing. Simply rest as much as you can and remember to keep your voice hydrated and as lubricated as possible.

Related Chapters

- Vocal Warm Ups

VOCAL WARM UPS

There are various vocal warm ups that any new or experienced singer can try. Each artist has their own way of practicing and making sure that they are ready for whatever the task at hand may be. In this section I will explain some basic vocal warm ups that need to be included in your daily routine when you are learning or even recording anything.

Any sort of singing is taxing on your vocal cords, and doing vocal warm ups will help your vocal cords not be as strained and help along the healing process if you do end up somehow damaging them. When you warm up your vocal cords you will also be able to sing better and extend your range far more than you think you can. While these warm ups won't immediately make you a better singer, they will help you gauge how far you can push yourself.

Here I will cover nine different vocal warm up techniques. You can do one of them over and over during your warm up process or try to do all of them. I recommend doing vocal warm up exercises for about 15 minutes. This will ensure that you are ready for any of the basics. If you do however feel the need to, you can do vocal exercises for up to 20 minutes but anything less than 10 minutes will not be sufficient and you may end up hurting yourself.

Yawn-Sigh Warm up

This technique is one of the easier techniques that can be used during your vocal warm ups. For this warm up you will inhale deeply through your nose, keeping your mouth closed, similar to how you would a yawn, and then slowly exhale, through your nose, like a sigh. This allows you voice relaxation and improved range.

Humming

Like the first vocal warm up, this is extremely easy, and classified as one of the easiest and best vocal warm ups for any level of singer. This warm up doesn't put any strain on your vocal cords at all, which makes it even better. Simply press the tip of our tongue to the back of your front teeth and hum. During the process of humming you can move up and down the major scale, being sure to keep your mouth closed as you hum.

Vocal Straws

These vocal warm ups are amazing for both beginners and intermediate singers. For this exercise you will however need a single item, a straw. To do this simply take your straw and place it between your lips and hum through it. The best way to do this is to start at the lowest range possible for you and to hum higher in range and then humming lower again. Once this has been done a few times you can select your favorite song and hum that through the straw.

Another way to use this as a vocal warm up is to fill a glass halfway with some water, placing the straw in the water and slowly blowing bubbles. Now this will not be just random bubble blowing as you will have to control the bubbles in a humming motion, letting them follow the range or song you're humming.

Lip Buzzing

This is one of the most fun vocal warm ups in my opinion. They are super simple and often referred to as lip trilling. Most people will enjoy this vocal warm up more than the others since you get to make the exercise itself fun. Simply try and recreate a motorboat sound by blowing air through your lips and nose while you are trilling them together. You can simply start at the lowest possible range and push it higher and higher as you continue to warm up.

Tongue Trills

This vocal cord warm up is somewhat intermediate and some artists may struggle with it. While you can practice it and get it right, I suggest using this technique alongside other techniques in this list. To use this warm up technique you will have to curl your tongue all while rolling your r's as you go from the lowest range to the highest and then back down. It is perfectly okay to struggle with this technique, and as I mentioned, using this technique alongside others will help you in the long run. Don't be shy to practice this technique to help you get better at creating out of the ordinary sounds with your mouth.

Jaw Loosening

Dropping your jaw is important in singing, while most people don't realize this, it is important to know that you need to drop your jaw lower than normal to be able to sing. This allows you to create louder and stronger sounds, so it only makes sense to include an exercise that helps you accomplish this.

To do this, simply keep your mouth closed, and pretend to yawn. While you are doing this, trail the edge of your jawline until you feel the curved section just below your ear. The small section between your jaw and ear is the part that you need to drop. Be careful and observant here that you are not just dropping your chin.

Octave Pitch Gliding

With this vocal warm up you will be recreating sounds that are similar to the 'eee' or 'ohhh' sound, but the warm up part will be the part where you build up gliding through a two-octave pitch. Simply glide up and down while doing this, transitioning from your chest voice to your head voice.

Sirens

This vocal warm up is quite similar to the previous one. For this exercise you will create an 'ooo' sound that will rise from the lowest to highest pitch and then back down, mimicking the sound of a siren. This is a great warm up as it covers all the tones that can be found between notes.

Vocal Sliding

This is one of the more difficult techniques, and is commonly referred to as *portamento*. This word comes from the Italian vocal warm up that can be translated t0 "carrying something". As with the previous warm up, you will create the sound and move from the lowest range to the highest, but the difference will be that you do not sing any of the in between tones and notes.

It is important to do these exercises before even thinking of starting your singing practice, especially if you are looking at rock, metal, and opera genres, where there is even more strain on your vocal cords and larynx.

Vocal Cool Down

One of the final things to remember after every practice session is that as well as physical exercise it is important to do some cool down exercises for your voice. These exercises help your vocal cords relax after some strenuous exercise, similar to how you would cool down a muscle in your arm or chest after exerting some physical effort into it. You can simply do the same warm up exercises that have been discussed to help cool down your voice. The cool down period is just as important as the warm up, and it allows you to slowly let your voice settle back into normal activities like talking. Without warm ups and cool downs you run the risk of hurting and even tearing the vocal folds, leading to painful recovery and oftentimes surgery.

BREATHING FOR MORE ARTICULATE SINGING

Breathing and articulation is extremely important when you are singing, as this will help you create louder and better sounds. Being able to breathe more efficiently will allow you to widen your vocal range and put less strain on your vocal cords.

In this section I will cover two basic breathing techniques that will help you articulate a lot easier during practice sessions.

Diaphragm Singing

Breathing techniques are extremely important as they will help you avoid any injury on your vocal cords and voice. When we are normally breathing we tend to breathe from our chest, especially when it comes to basic tasks like talking and walking. However, when you are singing it is important to breathe through your diaphragm.

This will give your voice the benefits of more power, better control over your voice as well as a fuller sound and far more expressionist tone. It will also keep you from straining your voice.

To sing through your diaphragm simply relax your entire body, focus on staying relaxed and balanced during this process and let your weight lean slightly forward. This will allow you ample air and space to be able to belt out those loud notes.

Hisses on an Exhale

This breathing technique can also be used as a warm up technique as it teaches you better voice and diaphragm control. It will slowly teach you to expand your lungs more, allowing you to hold certain notes for longer without having to inhale during a verse.

This technique can be mastered by using three steps. These steps are important to master as they will allow you better breath in for longer counts and use your air wisely.

1. Make sure that you are standing up straight and that you are relaxed. This will allow you to create clear and concise sounds without repressing the sound in your chest. This will also allow you to use the diaphragm technique, allowing you to relax any tension and keep you from singing notes in the wrong key.
2. Slowly breathe in through your mouth, counting to five as you do this. It is important to note that breathing deeply should not let your chest expand or let your shoulders rise, your belly would need to expand for this to be considered a "singer's breath" which is what you are looking for in this step. This might take some time to accomplish so take your time.
3. Once you have achieved that you can exhale, while counting to nine. It is important to create a sound similar to a hissing sound, almost like it would sound in 'snake'. When you reach nine you should have let all the air out of your lungs. As with the second step it is important to keep in mind that this might take a while, so practice as much as you need to, there is no limit on how long you should be focusing on this.

All of these breathing and vocal techniques are important as they will allow you to better understand your capabilities as well as your capacity for singing. They will take time to master, and not everyone will be able to grasp the concepts from the start.

Simply take your time to go through each activity and technique and practice as much as you need to. For some it might take a few hours, and for others it might take a few days or weeks and that is perfectly fine. These techniques are important to understand and do correctly as any deviance from the skills might end up hurting you and your voice in the long run. Don't be afraid to try other techniques that you gather from other singers, or from guides and teachers that you come across. Different techniques work for different people, so feel free to play around and find what works for you and your voice.

VOCAL RANGE

Vocal range is the range where you are able to sing. It is important to know in which vocal range you fall into, as forcing your voice to do things you are unable to do will hurt you in the end. It is oftentimes difficult to find your own vocal range, especially if you are starting out by yourself, without a vocal coach. This is where the tools I mentioned in Chapter 1 come in handy. Having a pitch pipe and a tuner for a guitar will help you gauge and adjust your pitch and tone. These instruments will allow you to better gauge what your vocal range is.

Vocal range is split into six main classes. Each of these has its own arrangements and structures. Knowing your range is important as it will allow you to better gauge what artists create similar music to you and what type of genre you will fit best into. While you can swap and change genres, and I do suggest trying out as much as you can, it is important to remember that not everyone will always be able to sing every range there is, and forcing yourself to sing a certain pitch higher or lower than you naturally can will cause irritation and strain on your body and voice.

The six different range classes are classified as follows:

1. Bass
2. Baritone
3. Tenor
4. Alto
5. Mezzo-Soprano
6. Soprano

These classes each have their own way of being identified and controlled, and various singers fall in multiple categories. In the following section I will cover what the vocal ranges are for each of these groups and I will add various artists as indicators of the type of sound they create.

Each of these ranges will be compared to the keys that can be found on a piano. I will be covering basic music notation in the next chapter.

The first three of these are generally found to be male voice ranges while the latter three are found to be more female ranges, but ever so often you will find that a male can sing a higher range and a female can sing a lower range.

Bass Range

The bass range will always be the lowest range possible and generally ranges from C2 to E4.

Popular singers that have a bass range are as follows:

- Barry White
- Johnny Cash

Baritone Range

The baritone range is slightly higher and falls between F2 and G4. These ranges are generally found in male voices.

Popular singers that have a baritone range are as follows:

- Chris Cornell
- David Bowie
- Elvis Presley

Tenor Range

Tenor ranges are higher than baritone ranges. The tenor range is generally from B2 to C5, and anything about C5 would be considered a falsetto.

Popular singers that fall in the tenor range are as follows:

- Bruno Mars
- Freddie Mercury
- Prince

Alto Range

The alto range is the lowest female range, similar to the base range, however these are commonly found in women. The alto range stretches from C#3 to E5.

Popular singers that are in the alto range are as follows:

- Cher
- Lana Del Rey
- Amy Winehouse

Mezzo-Soprano Range

The mezzo-soprano range is the middle of the ranges and falls between F3 and G#5.

Popular singers that fall in the mezzo-soprano range is as follows:

- Janis Joplin
- Alanis Morisette
- Lady Gaga

Soprano Range

The soprano range is the highest of the six ranges and spans from B3 to C6.

Popular singers that fall in the soprano range are as follows:

- Billie Eilish
- Whitey Houston
- Christina Aguilera

These are only the six main classifications and there are various other classifications that can be found within these six ranges. It is also not the end of the world if you do not fully fall into one of the six groupings. It is perfectly fine and you can go about genre selection however you want.

In the following section I will cover how to find your own range. There, I will take you step by step through the process, but please be aware that you will need to have a piano, whether a real one, electric one, or an online one to be able to do this.

Finding your Range

Finding your range is important as it will allow you to find the perfect genre for you and your voice. While it will be better for you to sing within a certain genre if you have a small range nothing can stop you from trying different genres and finding different styles. You may realize that certain things you are trying will help you better fall into another genre, allowing you more freedom.

Moving on to the actual range finding stage. This process might take you a while and you might struggle at first to find your perfect range but as with anything else, taking your time and trying multiple times will help. The process can be broken down into four different steps. I will explain each step thoroughly, as well as give you the help you need to find an artist that is similar to you in range to be able to better understand the sound you can create with practice and upskilling.

The following steps are the ones that you can use to find your range. Follow the steps to figure out what your perfect range will be. This process is not fool-proof, and your range might change somewhat if you find a vocal coach who has a more precise range finding method.

Step 1:

It is important to note that your singing voice is a bolder, more expanded version of your talking voice. Simply start humming, in a relaxed and calm manner, and while you are humming, hit the piano notes until you find one of them that sounds similar enough in sound to the one you are making while you are humming.

Step 2:

The following step is only a way to warm up your vocal folds and not a way to test your range. Take your time with this step, as it will take a while to warm up. Take a deep 'singer's' breath, expanding your stomach rather than letting it fill your chest. Slowly start doing a siren sound, and slowly build it up louder and louder. Do this a few times over until your voice is warmed up and then movie on to step three.

Step 3:

Refer back to the first note you hummed that sounded similar to the piano note you played. Simply follow the humming sound downward in a 'zah' method with the five general notes you know. Once you have done that, you can take half note steps down until you find a note that strains your voice. It is important to note that if your throat starts hurting or aching that you need to stop as this will cause strain. Once you have found the note where your voice starts to strain, you can mark this as the lowest your range will go.

Step 4:

This is the final step in finding your range. You will do something similar in this step as you did in the last step. Start humming at the base note and hum in a 'zee' way, this time, humming upwards in five note intervals. Once this has been done, you can hum in half-note intervals until you find a note that becomes too difficult to hum. That will be the highest note that you can possibly sing. This will allow you to have a rough estimate of what your range will be.

It is important to note that forcing notes will not be helpful and belting out sounds won't help you in the long run. You might come across some notes that will 'break' your voice. Notes are considered broken if you can sing the note before and after that specific note. This is normal and perfectly okay, and you can choose to avoid these notes or if you want to learn how to sing these notes in a healthy manner.

Learning what your pitch and vocal range is will allow you to create a better and fuller quality sound. Notes that are missed or considered broken can always be refined and focused on later on in your journey. But for now finding your vocal range and refining the notes that you are able to sing should be your main goal. This will help you track your progress far easier than you think. Once you get a vocal coach you can let them know which notes you can comfortably sing and which seem broken, letting them guide you down the right path to learn notes not entirely in your range.

GENRE SELECTION

Now that you have gone through the process of figuring out what and how your vocal range works you can finally move on to finding your genre. While a decade or two ago there were only a few genres to choose from, the last couple of years music has drastically changed and finding a genre that is to your liking has become far easier to discern than one might think.

The genre list has grown from jazz, pop and funk to an ever growing list of musical paths that will each take you on their own journey. This is one of the most exciting and most intense sections when you come into singing. There are hundreds of options to choose from, and being able to try more than one genre should definitely be something that you are considering!

The best possible way to move forward from here is to do your research on all the different genres that you are interested in and enjoy listening to. It is definitely difficult to just look at a list of genres and pick a single one that you will be expected to master in the next year or two. I suggest taking your time and researching genres that you have fallen in love with before.

It is important to remember that you do not have to be stuck with one single genre for years and years to come. As with anything in life, as you get older and grow, your skills and techniques will change and adapt and along with that your interest in music will also change, so it is only normal that you will want to change and adapt your own musical talents and enjoyments.

The easiest way to try and find something that will work for you is to pen down three or four genres that you enjoy. Whether it is jazz, punk, pop or hip hop. Once you have selected the few that you enjoy, take a moment to write down what you like about each genre and what you do not like about that specific genre. See this exercise as a sort of pros and cons list, helping you list out why you should and should not pick a certain genre.

Now that you have done that, try and eliminate one or two of the options. You do not have to do this, but if there is a genre you don't particularly connect with now that you have gone through these lists, then eliminate it from your list and move forwards. Now comes the fun part. Find multiple artists from each genre and find your favorite song from that artist. Doing this will make this part of the experience the most fun. Once you have done that, find the sheet music for it. There are various platforms where you can simply type in the artist and song name and the sheet music and notation will be generated for you.

The best way to find out what genre you enjoy, I have found, is to play that song and record yourself singing it, try and stay as close to the tone and pitch that the artist is, without letting the note fall flat. As a newbie this will be difficult and exhausting, especially in the beginning but this will be your jumping off point. Listening to the track back will allow you to hear if your range falls off entirely or if you only need some practice.

Never be afraid to try anything new, even if it is a genre that you happen upon while researching some artists. Sometimes you just stumble across a song that moves your soul, and you know that this is the type of experience you want to create for audiences and that is perfectly fine.

It is important to remember that you are only starting out and forcing yourself too much might make things more difficult in the long run. Give yourself time and patience as you work through different genres. Having a vocal coach here would be amazing as they would be able to guide you in the best possible direction when it comes to genre selection, but seeing as it is just you, be cool and calm and master one technique and skill before moving on to the next. Slow and steady wins the race as they say.

Genre Groupings

In this section I will list a few genres and their sub-genres to allow you to gauge the reality of what is actually looming ahead when you pick a genre.

Alternative

- College Rock
- New Wave

Blues

- British Blues
- Country Blues

Classical

- Ballet
- Baroque

Country

- Bluegrass
- Country Rock

Dance

- Dubstep
- Electro Swing

Folk

- British Folk Revival
- Indie Folk

Hip-Hop

- Alternative Rap
- Dirty South

Holiday

Indie Pop

Jazz

- Contemporary Jazz
- Dixieland

K-Pop

Metal

- Black Metal
- Doom Metal

Opera

Pop

- Adult Contemporary
- Pop Punk

R&B/Soul

- Motown
- Neo-Soul

Rock

- AfroPunk
- Cock Rock

Vocal

- A capella
- Vocal Jazz

These are not the only genres that one can find, and each of these main genres most definitely have more than just the two sub-genres that you can find here. Do not rush yourself, and take your time when finding your genre and sound.

HARMONY, RHYTHM, AND MELODY

Understanding music theory and the information it gives you regarding the music you wish to learn will help you better understand how the sounds are created and how they are meant to be used. This will help you better analyze any other genre of music and make it easier to create your own music.

This will also allow you to better communicate in the wonderful language of music. This knowledge will allow you to better compose and comprehend even the most intense and busy compositions. Music theory also allows you to better understand the harmony, melody and scales.

Music theory can be split into three overarching concepts and disciplines. These three fundamentals are the base or building blocks of any musical composition. If you understand these three building blocks and the impact they have on any musical composition, your journey will become far easier to do.

These three building blocks are as follows:

1. Harmony
2. Melody
3. Rhythm

Harmony

Harmony is the coming together of different notes and sounds to create a new sound. These sounds and notes are arranged in such a way that they harmonize and create a pleasing and wonderful sound.

Chord progressions and their partner chords are considered harmonies, as playing them together creates a pleasing and complementary sound. You can also add vocals to these cords to create a better harmony. Other examples of harmonies can be a choir, simply because bringing a group of vocals together and creating a pleasant sound is called a harmony.

Harmonies can be split into two branching categories. While harmonies are made to be pleasant, sometimes you might find that the sound clashes and does not create a pleasant sound at all.

Unharmonious groupings are called dissonant harmonies, and are often found when notes are played together that don't mesh well together. The cords in these groupings become unstable and the intervals do not fall together perfectly. You commonly find dissonant harmonies within the second, seventh and ninth intervals.

Harmonious groupings on the other hand are called consonant harmonies, and are stable and enjoyable sounds. These cords generally transition far more smoothly than dissonant harmonies and can be found in the unison, thirds, fifths, and octave intervals.

While it is not always desirable to use dissonant harmonies, they can be used alongside consonant harmonies to create a far more interesting and intriguing sound than just bunching together consonant harmonies.

Melody

Melodies are used to create musical phrases in succession, and is often the part that's most recognizable and the most memorable because of its repeating aspects. Like harmonies, melodies can be created through vocal phrases or musical phrases in succession.

It is important to remember that melodies often have two or more notes that are harmonious and pleasing that are repeated to create the melody. Most popular tracks also include multiple melodies that are strung together to create a harmonious track.

Melodies can be split into two elements: pitch and rhythm. Both of these are important and play significant roles in the creation of a truly harmonious and wonderful track.

Pitch will dictate how low or high the melody will be, and oftentimes the pitch is arranged in a step sort of manner to create an ascending or descending melody.

Rhythm on the other hand dictates how long and each pitch section will last. Most of these pitch sections are divided into beat divisions, most commonly half notes, quarter notes, as well as triplets. These divisions will dictate how long the pitch step lasts before moving on to the next pitch step.

Melody can also be split into two different melodic motions. This is done to dictate the tempo of the melody.

Conjunct motion will be used when the notes are moved by a full or half a step. Conjunct motion is generally used because it is the more natural way of singing and talking. Conjunct motion is also used when there are smaller steps like quarter note steps.

Disjunct motion is therefore used when there are enlarged steps. These larger steps will make the song difficult to sing and play as it will create a choppy sound and a less smooth singing sound. Like consonant and dissonant harmony, most artists use conjunct and disjunct motion together to create more intriguing and exciting sounds and tracks.

Rhythm

Rhythm is one of the most important parts of any musical track, whether it has vocals or not, and what makes it so amazing is the fact that rhythm can be split into two different divisions, depending on the section of vocals and music it covers in a track. Rhythm can be seen as the repeating of movements and silences in a song, and helps us keep track of time, but it can also be used to describe the patterning that's found in both the strong and weak notes within a composition. These repeating patterns can be created with percussion, instruments as well as vocals.

Rhythm can and oftentimes is composed from seven different elements. These elements will always be musical and rhythmic based. These seven elements are as follows:

1. Beat

Beats are generally used when there is a repeating pulse or base sound that creates the underlying musical patterns.

2. Meter

Meter is generally used to portray the weak and strong beats in a musical track.

3. Time Signature

The time signature measures the number of beats per minute that can be found in the tempo.

4. Tempo (BPM)

The tempo (beats per minute) will indicate how fast or how slow the entire track will be.

5. Strong and Weak Beats

Strong beats can be described as the downbeats, and the weak beats can be described as the offbeats that are found between the downbeats.

6. Syncopation

Syncopation is generally rhythms that would lay emphasis on the offbeats that are found between the downbeats.

7. Accents

Generally, when you see and work with accents in the rhythm category they refer to the emphasis that has been placed on notes. It can also refer to how intense a note is played.

Having a basic understanding of what rhythm can do for you and for the track you want to create will allow you to create amazing harmonies and melodies. It is also one of the most important things to understand as rhythm is the backbone for any track, giving both structure and pulse to the track.

MUSIC THEORY FUNDAMENTALS

Knowing the fundamentals for music theory will allow you to better understand the timing, notation, and basic rhythm of any track, in turn making it easier to learn a new song, and making it even easier to learn how to sing.

Notes and Intervals

It is best to know how notes relay to piano keys, especially since most of the references are mostly made to use with the companion of a piano or keyboard. Relating the piano keys to notes will help you learn to read music much quicker.

The next section will cover how the melody and harmony interact with each other and show how the available notes relate. Before moving on I will include a diagram of all the notes and how they relate to each other on their corresponding piano keys.

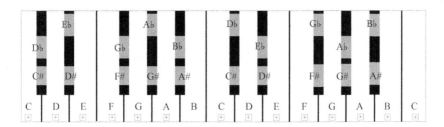

In the above diagram you can see the 12 notes, or key signatures, that are used as the building blocks for any and all music creation. These notes will be repeated upwards and downwards in octaves.

It is important to note that the musical alphabet only has seven different base notes; namely A through G. These base notes are then split into the 12 notes that you can see above.

The seven notes can be classified as follows:

- A
- A♯ / B♭
- B
- C
- C♯ /D♭
- D
- D♯ / E♭
- E
- F
- F♯ /G♭
- G
- G♯ /A♭

It is important to note the notation next to the notes. The white keys on the piano represent the normal notes and only using these during a composition will leave your composition in A Minor or C Major.

The black keys on a piano are the flat and sharp keys.

Musical notation for flat notes will look like this: ♭

Whereas musical notation for sharp notes will look like this: ♯

Thus, when you compose in both the white and black keys you will be able to compose a track that is rich in both flat and sharp notes as well as any other available signatures that can be found.

Intervals

Intervals can be classified as the distance between different notes. These distances are generally measured between two notes and are measured by half steps, whole steps as well as their position on the scale.

Steps are calculated in the following way:

- Half step intervals are considered to be semitones
- Whole step intervals are considered to be two semitones
- Two half steps will then create a whole step.

It is important to remember that the intervals are considered to be the basis and foundation of both the harmony and the melody. This will be evident when you play two notes simultaneously, creating a harmonious interval with cords or when you play various single notes in succession, making melodic intervals with the melodies.

Intervals are generally described by numbers (also known as the distance) and their prefixes (also known as their quality). Their numbers would represent the half-steps that can be found between two notes. Generally the numbers (or distance of half-steps) is generally classified as follows: 1st (unison), 2nd, 3rd, 4th, 5th, 6th, 7th, and 8th (octave).

Intervals can also be described using their prefixes, the prefix thus describes the quality of the note. These prefixes are classified as follows: major (M), minor (m), perfect (P), augmented (A), and diminished (d).

Octaves and Signatures

Octaves are an important part of any composition. They lay out the lowest and highest pitch that can be found from a specific note. The easiest way to differentiate between notes is using an octave. Consider a note like C1, the octave up from C1 will then be C2, and the octave down from C1 will be C0.

These octave jumps can be found when you double the frequency of the first note. The 12 semitones that are found in an octave will always repeat in the exact same order, no matter what the range of hearing is.

Key signatures are used to tell us whether or not a note will be sharp, or flat.

As mentioned before there are 12 key signatures, all of them deriving from the 12 notes that we use throughout composition. Key signatures are also used to identify the entire key for a song.

If you find that a song has an A minor key, most of the note composition and key signatures will come from the A minor scale. Scales will be more thoroughly discussed in the next section.

Scales and Modes

The scales in music are the literal building blocks for any and all musical compositions, whether it is vocal or instrumental in nature. In this section I will cover the scale degree, the music modes that one can find, as well as the most common scales used in everyday sound.

As we all know, scales are used to classify the interval relationships between descending and ascending notes, allowing us to gauge the scales that will be used for a project.

While we work mainly with major and minor scales, there are also other types of scales that can be used in your composition. Major scales are mainly used with happy sounding tracks, as the sounds will be far more cheerful and bright. On the opposite of that we find minor scales that are mainly used for more somber emotional tracks. While the minor scales include the 12 natural scales, minor scales also have three different variations mainly; natural, harmonic and melodic, each serving a different function.

Scale degrees play another important role when it comes to music creation and composition. Each scale has a functionality and those functionalities are what we call scale degrees. They serve as reference to the functionality and the tension that it can create within a certain composition.

Scale degrees are split into seven different degrees:

- 1st will be the Tonic scale degree

- 2nd will be the Supertonic scale degree
- 3rd will be the Mediant scale degree
- 4th will be the Subdominant scale degree
- 5th will be the Dominant scale degree
- 6th will be the Submediant scale degree
- 7th will be the Leading Tone degree.

Each of these scale degrees will change the tension in a composition, and remembering what they each do is difficult. Later in this section, I will give a basic table that will help describe what each tone degree does.

Scale degrees act as parent scales for musical modes. Similar to the seven scale degrees there are seven musical modes, each responsible for a different variant than the parent scale it comes from. The difference between the parent scale and the musical mode will be the root note that is used when starting the scale. This subtle change can affect the entire composition and feeling surrounding the track.

Musical modes are generally classified and distinguished in the following ways:

- **I - Ionian** which is a major scale
- **ii - Dorian** which is considered a major scale that starts on the second degree scale.
- **iii - Phrygian** which is a major scale that starts on the third degree scale.
- **IV - Lydian** which is a major scale that starts on the fourth degree scale.
- **V - Mixolydian** which is a major scale that starts on the fifth degree scale.
- **vi - Aeolian** which can be a natural minor or major scale that starts on the sixth degree scale.
- **vii - Locrian** which is a major scale that starts on the seventh degree scale.

In the following table you will see how these musical modes and seven scale degrees interact. While it is difficult learning this, I feel that it is important to know the basics surrounding these transitions and how they affect sound, especially because this will help your understanding when it comes to note and scale changes in difficult tracks.

Key	Ionian	Dorian	Phrygian	Lydian	Mixolydian	Aeolian	Locrian
C Major	C	D	E	F	G	A	B
G Major	G	A	B	C	D	E	F♯
D Major	D	E	F♯	G	A	B	C♯
A Major	A	B	C♯	D	E	F♯	G♯
E Major	E	F♯	G♯	A	B	C♯	D♯
B Major	B	C♯	D♯	E	F♯	G♯	A♯
F Major	F	G	A	B♭	C	D	E
B♭ Major	B♭	C	D	E♭	F	G	A
E♭ Major	E♭	F	G	A♭	B♭	C	D
A♭ Major	A♭	B♭	C	D♭	E♭	F	G
D♭ Major	D♭	E♭	F	G♭	A♭	B♭	C
G♭ Major	G♭	A♭	B♭	C♭	D♭	E♭	F
Roman Numeral Major	i	ii	iii	iv	v	vi	vii dim

PART II

Part two of this guide will cover more in depth vocal exercises and tutorials, helping you build up your vocal and performance abilities as you move forwards in your journey.

Here, I will also cover vocal coaching as well as tools of the trade that every future artist should consider investing or using.

YOUR VOCAL EXERCISE ROUTINE

Having an exercise routine will help your practice become a smooth process that you can do no matter where you are. It will become second nature for you and rehearsals and auditions will become a piece of cake.

Singing, like every other activity in the world, is not something that you can just up and do out of nowhere. Even if you have natural talent, working hard and pushing through long rehearsal days will have to become the norm for you. Practicing and doing it in the right way is extremely important and being consistent will only help your progress in the long run. Let's face it, no one wants to struggle through long rehearsals and even longer practice sessions, but if you work hard at it and stay consistent, it will all pay off in the end.

When you think of a practice session, you should know that a normal session includes vocal warm ups as well as physical warm ups, vocal exercises that will not only improve but better your tone, articulation, breathing and range. These sessions also generally include a section where you will apply the skills you learned during your vocal exercises to a song of your choosing. Practice and rehearsals are important and oftentimes the rehearsals are far more enjoyable since you get to play around with sounds and truly find your own sound, the thing that makes you unique. In this chapter I will cover a basic exercise program that can be followed by anyone, that starts with both vocal and physical warm ups, vocal exercises, putting those exercises into practice, and then cool down exercises.

Before Practice Starts

It is important to be prepared for practice sessions, whether you only have 30 minutes to practice or you have an entire afternoon. It is important that you make your practice sessions a routine that you can follow no matter where you go. I would suggest setting up times every second day for practice, make out an hour or two hours in your diary purely for practice and stick to those set times. The best way to get into a routine is to set constant reminders for yourself.

You will need various items when you are practicing, whether it is only for 30 minutes or an entire hour, but make time to set up everything beforehand. Especially if you know you only have a short period of time. You don't want to spend 15 minutes gathering everything you need and then spending 10 minutes warming up only to have your gym reminder or class reminder interrupt you five minutes into the practice.

Think about setting a reminder for 10 to 15 minutes before a practice and set up everything you may need, that way you can relax for a few seconds before your practice starts and you know you won't be rushing yourself and making yourself anxious. Besides the normal items you may need to practice I suggest also keeping a journal of how you are progressing and how practice sessions are going. Especially if you are not working with a vocal coach.

The following items are things I recommend every single aspiring singer should have during their practice times:

1. Keyboard or piano
2. Pitch Pipe
3. Metronome
4. Recorder or your phone for recording
5. Sheet Music and a pencil
6. Mirror
7. Notebook or Diary
8. Water

Each of these items serves an important role during practice sessions and each of them will help you better understand and progress in sessions. The piano or keyboard will allow you to stay in tune when you are struggling to keep track of the notation. The pitch pipe as explained before will help you hear the pitch you need t0 start off with when you start practicing. Your metronome will keep count of the tempo and BPM, allowing you to stay on track and time during a fast or slower paced track. Recording yourself will help you find where you are falling flat or making mistakes. Be sure to record yourself and listen back to it to give yourself an idea of what you should focus on in the next session.

Your sheet music, pencil and diary is a way for you to keep track of all the changes and issues you are going through. You might realize that the song of your choosing has a pitch that's a little too high for you but you can tone down the pitch and still make it sound harmonious. A mirror will help you see when you are not enunciating or making small breathing mistakes during practice, and last but not least, water for hydration.

Practice Session

Here I will cover the small routine that you can alter to help yourself grow and improve.

When you are warming up, whether it is your vocal cords or your body, it is important to remember that warming up will allow your body to perform in better conditions. In this section I will cover both physical exercises that will help you reach that peak as well as vocal exercises that can be incorporated into your practice routine to help you perform on a higher level.

When you are focusing on your body's physical warm up, you do not need to spend 20 minutes warming up. You can do a few simple movements and stretches that will help your upper body relax and stay calm during your practice session before moving on to your vocal exercises. One of the best ways to know if your body is fully warmed up, is when you realize that your body fully engages in the activity of singing. Oftentimes you may find that the 10 minutes you set aside for physical warm ups aren't enough, and that's fine; simply spend a few extra minutes repeating the activities and then move on to vocal warm ups. You may also find that the opposite is true, that after about five minutes you feel your body ready to engage in the session, simply spend a few extra seconds finishing the exercise you are on and then move on to vocal preparations. You know your body best, so do what feels natural and what works for you.

Physical Warm Ups

Stretching and preparing your body physically for any short or long session you will be engaging in will be important, like your voice, and any other muscles you want them to be prepared for the breathing changes and movement change you are going to be attempting.

The stretching routine I suggest starts at your head and slowly works down to your toes, taking about 10 minutes. I will cover this stretching routine in the following steps.

It is important to take slow and deep breaths through the entire stretching session.

No matter which step you are at, focus on breathing deeply in and out, letting your body get used to the breathing changes.

Step 1:

The first step is to close your eyes, and slowly shake away any stiffness you may have from the day. Slowly inhale and exhale as you do this, making sure to move each and every joint possible.

Step 2:

Now that your joints are feeling a little more relaxed, look straight ahead, and slowly tilt your head down, letting your neck muscles slowly stretch with you, inhale and exhale slowly, letting your neck stretch more on each exhale. Once you have done this a couple of times, you can slowly start bringing your head back.

Now that the neck muscles are a little more lucid, slowly turn your chin to your left shoulder, and keep your chin as close to your chest as possible. Without pressing your chin against your chest, slowly rotate your chin to the right side. Repeat this one or two times until you feel your neck muscles become a little less tight. Be careful not to roll your head back, as some injuries may incur if this movement is done wrong.

Here we will continue stretching our neck muscles. Slowly lower your left ear to your left shoulder, do so while inhaling and exhaling, wait a few seconds and on the next exhale lower your ear a little more. Repeat this for this action a few times and then for the right side as well.

Step 3:

Now that the neck muscles are relaxed we can move on to your facial muscles. This is a simple one. Simply tense and scrunch up all the muscles in your face and then relax them. Do this multiple times before moving on to the next section of this step.

Once you have relaxed the muscles in your face you can now focus on stretching your tongue. Funny enough this will feel awkward and strange but this really helps you in the long run. For this exercise you will stick your tongue out as far as you can and then move it back in. It is okay to lick your lips while doing this.

Step 4:

Now we can move on to your shoulders and hands. First start off with your shoulders. Tighten your shoulder muscles by pushing them up and then relax them by letting them down again. Be careful not to use your chest for this motion.

Now we can move on to your arms, use the right arm and lift it vertically into the air, until it is straight up beside you, slowly circle your arm around, this way moving your shoulders and your arm. Remember to wiggle your fingers while you do this. Do this for a couple of seconds and then switch to the opposite arm.

Step 5:

This exercise will stretch your side muscles. It is important as you will be pushing your body a little more than it is used to. Slowly reach your right hand towards your left side, letting it reach over your head and stay like that for a few seconds before standing upright again. Do this a few times before swapping to the other side.

Step 6:

This exercise will target your hips and legs. Many female artists have found that their stress is held in their hips. So take a moment to rock your hips back and forth as much as you need, and then slowly make circles with your hips. Remember to breathe while you do this.

Now we can move on to the feet and legs. Slowly push yourself up onto your toes and then slowly lower yourself back onto the flats of your feet. Try to do this exercise without holding on to anything. If you find that your balance is lacking you can opt to hold onto a chair or rest one hand against a wall for support.

Step 7:

This is the final step before we can move on to vocal exercises. Take a deep breath and shake away the last nerves and any stiffness you may have and then close your eyes, taking a few deep breaths before moving on to the vocal exercises.

These exercises will help you feel refreshed and focused since your heart rate went up and got your blood pumping a little faster. Now you can finally move on to the type of vocal exercises you would like to try.

Vocal Warm Ups

Vocal exercises have been covered in the beginner section but I will include some extra information in this section.

Vocal warm ups are extremely important as they will help your vocal cords and throat prepare for the practice you are about to go through. Without any sort of warm up you run the risk of permanently damaging your vocal cords, so be sure to take the time to warm them up; they work like any other muscle and a good warm up will give you a much better workout.

You can use a myriad of different vocal warm up techniques and each artist does their own thing, some follow a simple rhyme they were taught while others hum their favorite song as they stretch their arms. It is ultimately up to you. There are nine amazing techniques in Chapter 2 that you can adapt and change as you see fit.

Now that your warm up has finished you can finally move on to vocal exercises.

Vocal Exercises

Each vocal artist has a different voice and thus does different types of vocal exercises, not to mention that different exercises work better for different types of genres and that is definitely something that you want to keep in mind while you are working on figuring out what vocal exercises will be the best for you.

Here, I will cover information on basic vocal exercises that almost anyone can use in their routines to help them along their journey. It is important to remember that any vocal exercise can be used, but I would suggest making sure that the exercise you do choose to do is something that you can actually get through.

I would suggest looking up a few vocal exercises, or even using the ones in the vocal warm up section (see Chapter 2) for this purpose.

It is important to use your diary when doing vocal exercises; being able to take notes will help you greatly, especially during the exercise portion. I would suggest making notes on the exercises you wish to practice and work on during a session and going through the explanation and instructions beforehand so you don't spend too much time having to worry about how you are supposed to do the exercise. When you are finished with your exercise, make notes on what worked well for you and what did not, make sure to write any comments on things you might wanna change for the next week.

Another thing you want to consider is the difficulty level of the exercises that you choose, picking something you are unable to do as a beginner will make the experience unenjoyable and might deter you from continuing, so be careful to not pick up something too difficult when you are picking exercises.

One of the most important things to remember is that no matter your skill level or natural talent, a hobby or career like singing takes time and dedication. You need to take time to practice; it won't just happen overnight and spending a few hours a month on something minor, like a single warm up exercise, won't help you either. You have all the tools and information at your fingertips, you just need to be dedicated enough to take time out every day and practice all the things you need to practice, and if you are struggling ask for help, whether it is from a friend or an online community. There are a lot of resources out there, don't be afraid to ask for help.

Practice Songs

You have gone through the process of warming up, both physically and vocally, and you spent the last 30 minutes doing vocal exercises, and now you get to put those exercises into practice. You now get to pick a song and make it your own.

Be sure that the song you pick falls in your genre and vocal range, you do not want to put in hours upon hours of work and then find out that the cover of your favorite song is vastly different than the original and you cannot even begin to fathom how to sing the original.

Find a song that you really enjoy and feel like you would connect with, and spend some time practicing the lyrics and listening to the music while you are busy with other tasks. This will help you pick up on small musical cues for certain note and pitch changes.

Make sure that you are using the vocal exercises that you worked so hard on to get better at singing this particular song. It is important that your practice lines up with the final day of practice when you finally move on to singing the song you've been wanting to sing for so long.

It might take you a few tries to get the timing, pitch and range accurate but like with anything in the music industry, practice makes perfect. This is the perfect time to use your recorder. Record yourself singing the song and listen to it. Be sure to make notes on any sections you felt were flat or where it seemed like you were missing notes. Make notes on anything you want to improve on in the coming week and then move forwards from here.

Once you have finished your exercises, it is important to take a few minutes to do some vocal cool down exercises. Simply repeat the vocal exercises you used in the beginning. Like with normal muscles, doing some basic cool down exercises will help your vocal muscles relax after putting it through the exercises you did. Remember to hydrate and rest your voice, at least once a week. Not doing so would be bad for your voice, so be sure to rest.

It is important to note that all the practice you put in will consistently improve you, if you are doing it right. Like with physical exercise you will get tired and that is normal, especially at the beginning. Be sure to take sufficient breaks, and most of all remember that singing while you are in pain may result in permanent damage and nobody wants that.

It is going to take time to get better, even if you consistently put in the work, but don't be too hard on yourself; you are new to all of this and forcing yourself will not fix or magically make you better.

Related Chapters:

- Voice Health
- Vocal Warm Ups
- Vocal Range

GENRE REQUIREMENTS

Each genre has its own requirements, and sometimes you might meet those requirements while other times you will not meet those requirements, and that is absolutely okay. Being able to learn and change your singing style is an option but the best way to create a healthy and good relationship with singing is to be able to have a long lasting career. This section can also be linked with Chapter 3's genre selection as I will cover basic genres and what requirements you might need for these basic genres.

Each of these genres have their own unique style and tempo and being able to find something you are comfortable and familiar with is important, but don't feel too boxed in by these requirements as each of these have other aspects that are not mentioned here. There are also hundreds of other genres that can be looked into. I have opted to cover these genres as they are the most popular types of genres and a lot of their aspects are overarching when it comes to genres that are somewhat similar. For example rock, pop and pop-rock all have similar requirements but are seen as three completely different genres.

Take your time to discover what works for you and your voice and do not force yourself into a genre that you won't enjoy for a while. And if all else fails, remember that nothing is stopping you from starting out and trying something new.

In this section I will be covering two criteria for each genre: the type of sound that is created and the technique that will create that type of sound. I will also include a few other artists that are similar.

Country

Country music is generally sung more by male artists, but in the last decade or two we have seen more and more female artists tackle the country music scene. This type of music typically makes you think of old farm roads and typical country sounds make you long for a love you lost years ago or a good night out with the boys.

It is common that the sounds are quite different when compared to other types of genres and most of the songs have an entire story to tell.

Country sound generally is found to be slow starting, but in recent years I have found that some of the country music is arching into pop music, similar sounds being created by both country and pop artists. Country music however focuses on creating an entire narrative for the listener, creating a feeling like an old friend is telling a story. You often also find that country singers have a twang in their sounds, making the country feeling even more evident.

Country singers don't focus too much on how they pronounce certain words and letters so try and focus on that. They generally have voices more made for slow singing, making the sound similar to a talking ballad. Be sure that you understand the balance between belting and using your chest voice as many country singers use belting instead of their chest voice during their songs.

There are so many country singers that are popular right now, but with the overarching genre I am going to stick to some classic recommendations like Johnny Cash, Trisha Yearwood, and Reba McEntire.

Pop-Rock

Pop-rock is one of my personal favorite genres, and I absolutely love the feeling it gives me. While I enjoy both pop and rock, the mix between the two really brings out the best of both worlds. Both these genres are very vocally demanding and keeping your vocals healthy is extremely important!

Solid technique is definitely a must when it comes to pop-rock. While some artists have mics that have pitch correction and reverb simulators, it is rare to find this in the pop-rock genre, as the fuzzy tone they wish to convey is something they want to keep as it adds to the overall sound. Most pop-rock artists also have a vibrato echo that often comes after the initial vocals. This is perfectly okay as well, and you don't need to worry about this too much.

Pop-rock artists are generally artists that sing and dance while they are on stage so being fit and healthy is definitely something you should consider when taking the pop-rock genre into consideration. In my opinion, the best way to actually gauge if you will be able to do this is to find your favorite pop song and sing and dance along. If you find that you struggle and would not want to put in the extra work for learning dances and changing your diet to get in shape, perhaps consider another genre. Most rock artists also create screaming sounds, more commonly known as growling. This is taxing on the vocal folds and the body. Be sure to do thorough research when taking the rock genre into consideration as you will definitely need a vocal coach to help you with resonance training to be able to make those sounds.

There are so many artists that can be mentioned here, especially because pop-rock is a mash up of two amazing genres. I recommend looking at the following artists if you are looking into the pop-rock genre: Billy Joel, Meatloaf and Rod Stewart.

Musical Theater

Musical theater is a lot different than just performing a song on a stage, it often goes along with acting and storytelling, much like with country, except you will rarely ever perform by yourself. There will almost always be a large group with you, performing alongside you. This genre is very intimidating at first, as those in this career need to know far more genre basics and sound creation with their vocals than normal artists that will be performing a single type of genre.

Being a musical theater artist will mean that you will have to create a conversational sound. Not something that sounds too much like it is an actual song. When you are part of a musical theater group you will need to understand how to adjust your vocals and sounds when you are using a handheld mic or if you are wearing a body mic. You will have to make adjustments to both your speech and your movement, thus not creating popping sounds nor making scratchy sounds on the mic because of your movements.

The techniques that musical theater artists use are very similar to those that opera singers use. Simply because they are creating open space sounds that are considered to be voice-dominated sounds. Musical theater artists however also use belting during their performances, so it is important to keep that in mind when you are looking to focus on musical theater.

Musical theater is a very broad genre, and different artists have different techniques so I will recommend a few more artists than with the previous genres so you can spend time thoroughly researching the topic and feeling. I suggest looking at artists like Kristin Chenoweth, Idina Menzel, John Raitt, Joel Grey ,and Gwen Verdon.

Jazz

Jazz is often a mix of other genre songs that are harmoniously put together to create something new, so if this is the type of music you enjoy then perhaps consider getting into jazz and the singing behind it. Jazz is generally created with a different tempo and rhythm than normal or musical theater sounds and very rarely do the singers stay note to note with the instrumentalists.

Jazz is considered to be a contemporary field of music, and very often compared to musical theater because of play styles and similarities. It is important to note that jazz is more focused on how the artist uses their voice in a similar way to an instrument. Instead of having lyrics written for the entire song, vocalists will often only sing certain syllables, being able to scat along with the music instead of singing the lyrics.

To be able to become a great jazz singer you will have to be able to keep track of any changes in the music and improvise sounds and changes along with the band members. Scatting is also a skill that most jazz singers often use during their performances so knowing how to utilize that to the best possible outcome will always be a win. While a decent sense of rhythm is required for most musical careers, it is even more so needed when you are a jazz singer, especially because the band members will create background music for the individual melody that you as vocalist will create and perform.

There are tons of jazz artists that you can find, and each of them has their own influences and governing rules, so while I will suggest some artists, I do suggest doing some research on your own. Look at artists like Bobby McFerrin, Ella Fitzgerald and Diana Krall.

Opera

Opera is an amazing genre that takes a lot of skill to accomplish. The training and rehearsals for opera is a lot more intense and generally a far longer process than traditional pop or rock training. The longer process might seem silly but this will just allow you to better refine and master your voice and what it can do for you and your future projects. While you do rarely find opera in English you will more often than not have to be able to sing in German, Italian, Russian or French, as most of the musical productions and opera productions are kept in their native tongue. Fluency is not needed, but understanding the basics for either one or two of these languages will help you in the long run if you consider becoming an opera singer.

Opera vocals generally consist of long singing phrases and very loud singing, as the artists need to be heard above the orchestra that will often play along with the production. It is important to note that even though the songs are much less complex, they do extend longer than normal lyrical vocals will and thus puts a little more strain on your voice and endurance.

The singing technique that most artists use is extremely important as the main performance will be how you relay the sound you are making. In opera singing, the technique where singers open their mouth wide and let their throat expand to let the sound out is called *bel canto*. You will definitely have to have endurance for this genre. The best way to grow your singing endurance is to practice, practice, and practice some more. Be sure that you can sing for up to four hours as some, if not most operas last between two and four hours at a time. There are of course breaks in between but the breaks are not nearly efficient enough to gather up all your energy for another round of singing. Voice health has never been as important as it is now.

There are quite a few opera artists that are amazing at their craft but I will share a variety of them so you can find a taste of everything. Look at artists like Renée Fleming, René Pape and Olga Borodina.

CHOIR TRAINING

How you want to train is an important thing to consider. As mentioned in the beginning, you might want to look into joining a choir, and this is not necessarily a bad thing. Being part of a choir is beneficial in various ways and can help your skills improve exponentially. Not necessarily in the way that you think but it is definitely something you should consider.

In this chapter I will cover the benefits of both joining a choir and the benefits of staying by yourself for the basics and getting a vocal coach later on. In the next chapter I will cover why you should consider getting a coach. For now, let's dive into why a choir would be good for you.

The Benefits of Joining a Choir

While it is not only beneficial in terms of helping you become more social and deal with stage fright, as well as any other social anxiety you might have, it also allows you to become a part of a community that wishes to do the same things you are doing. They want to enjoy their craft while also getting better and expanding their knowledge and improving their skills.

When you are a part of a choir, not only do you have to focus on staying on the correct note, and focus on the sections you have to sing but you also have to focus on listening to those around you. A piece of advice that was given to me years and years ago by a choir teacher stated that "If you cannot hear your neighbor next to you, then you are singing far too loudly." When you are part of a choir you have to consider that your loud vocals may drown out someone else's, and in turn you will cause the harmonies and melodies to get muddled and messy. This of course is not optimal at all. So being a part of a choir will teach you how to listen to yourself and to those around you, allowing you to better gauge your temp and volume. It will also allow you to gauge if the style of singing you are following is not exactly appropriate, and by simply listening for a few seconds you can find your rhythm again and get back to harmonizing like before.

Being able to feel the sound you are making seems silly. Who knows what the sound they are making feels like, but when you are a part of a choir this will become a skill that you can improve on and be able to use years and years later when you have become a solo artist yourself. Oftentimes in choirs because you are so intent on not over-shadowing or crushing the vocals of those around you, you might also struggle to hear yourself fully. It is during these times that you have to be able to feel the sound you are creating. While this sounds silly, you know your body and if you have been rehearsing you know what the sound is supposed to feel like in your throat, chest and mouth, and you will know when something is off. If this does happen simply tone it down a little, take a small breather and then fall back in. This will ultimately teach you more control over your voice and breathing, which is important no matter how you look at it.

Sometimes you will go from singing in a large auditorium to a small church hall and this will mean having to adjust the volume of your own voice to have the sound not bounce back constantly. Singing in a choir also helps you gauge this as those around you will have to adjust their volume as well. A simple and easy trick that you can do to test your voice and volume is to create a small cup around your ear, this technique will allow you a little more hearing ability in terms of your own voice and allow you gauge how much louder or softer you will have to sing.

Another benefit of joining a choir is the fact that your hearing will become much more sensitive, especially when it comes to your own voice. When you are rehearsing alone, you often time record your-self to pick up where you made mistakes, this trains your ear to certain sounds that your voice makes. Similarly this happens when you are training with a choir. When there are a group of people all singing together, your ear finds your voice and tries its best to isolate it. Being in a choir will allow you to practice this, allowing you to find small mistakes even if there are 45 people next to you singing a Christmas carol.

Getting to be social and to travel with a choir should purely be bonuses at this point. As I mentioned before, you might struggle with social anxiety and struggle to interact with people or you might have stage fright and dealing with that will help you in the long run. Being with a group allows you to make friends with those people, and knowing that you cannot just walk away because you have a whole group of people supporting you on stage next to you will help with that. Most choirs also travel within their cities, performing at various locations, some are even often asked to perform at large events or shows. This will allow you to see more places, without having to worry about major planning and budgeting as the choir will most probably have an administrator that does all the planning ahead of time.

It is common knowledge that various artists that are now popular all had some sort of social anxiety and did not enjoy performing in front of people. While there are artists that flourished in front of groups of people, I can definitely agree that performing in front of large crowds is daunting, and having people there with you will help your social anxiety and any jitters you might have. One may not think so, but even having one or two people supporting you during a performance makes things feel far less intense and stressful. The best way to overcome this is to slowly work your way up to singing solo before leaving the choir or moving on to something different.

Choir Singing vs Solo Singing

Here I will cover the differences between solo singing and choir singing. While each of these has their own perks it is definitely up to you to decide what you want to do. In this section I will highlight and discuss the five most important differences between singing in a choir and singing solo.

1. Vibrato

When you are a part of a choir you will oftentimes be prompted to sing without vibrato, while when you are singing solo you will most probably sing with vibrato. This is something that needs to be learned and practiced and if you can swap between the two effortlessly then why not.

2. Range vs Finding a Part

Choirs often have multiple people that sing in the same range, so more often than not you will be asked to fill a certain role, whereas singing solo will allow you to sing in whatever range you want, giving you far more freedom.

3. Volume Control

Singing in a choir means keeping a low volume so as not to overpower certain harmonies and melodies created by other singers. Being a solo artist means that you can comfortably sing as loud or as soft as you want and need to.

4. Resting Times

This is one of the more minor issues that I have found but sometimes choir practices tend to drag along a little longer, meaning you will have to stay standing for longer periods of time, being unable to rest. When you are a soloist, you can take small breaks whenever you want to.

5. Facial Expressions

This might seem silly but most of the time the choir director will let everyone know to keep their facial expressions as neutral as possible, only hoping to convey a singular emotion. On the opposite side of that argument, being a soloist means you can let your emotions show as much as you want and need.

The Choice is Yours

Considering all of the above information, it is still ultimately up to you if you want to join a choir or not. Both options have their pros and cons. Be sure to weigh up the options thoroughly before making a decision.

In the end this is something you love and want to do for years to come, and doing something that you do not particularly enjoy for the sake of doing it won't be the best choice. The music industry is a difficult one and you might end up doing something you never considered doing earlier, but be sure that no matter what you do what will work for you and make you more comfortable and happy.

Related Chapters:

- Voice Health

PROFESSIONAL COACHING

In this chapter I will cover the pros and cons of finding a professional coach. I will also give suggestions and information regarding ways on how to find the best coach as well as include some basic and common policies that can be found at most vocal coaching establishments, and I will include a section on the type of questions you should ask when you are looking at getting a vocal coach.

While you are going through this learning process, it is of course always important to consider professional help. Having a vocal coach will help you greatly, especially if you find the perfect coach for you in the beginning of your career. They will be able to help you estimate and gauge your range.

Another pro to having a vocal coach is having an actual date and time set for rehearsals. This will keep you from skipping practice sessions and just winging it when you do practice. While I do agree that getting a vocal coach is an investment, there are quite a few pros to having a professional help you on your journey.

While I understand that financially one cannot always afford a vocal coach, you could even opt to ask a friend or the local church choir director to help you out if you are in a pinch. Being a soloist is difficult, especially if you are new to all of this and you feel like you have been thrown into the deep end. Having someone there to support and help you work your way through everything always makes things easier.

It is however important to note that not each and every vocal coach is equal and not all of them carry your best interest at heart. It is extremely important to find a vocal coach that will carry your best interest at heart. It is also important to note that not all vocal coaches focus on all genres. You might have to find a second vocal coach after learning the basics that focuses on the genre you are looking for, especially if it is something more alternative like rock and metal genres where certain vocal sounds and singing might end up hurting you if you do it incorrectly.

Other options to consider is joining a group for vocal lessons. These options are often a little cheaper, but are lacking in personal attention, as group sessions are often split between you and five other students. Each school or coach of course has their own policies for groups and individuals but sending an email or calling to find out what their policies are can never be a bad thing.

Always be sure that you know what you want from a vocal coach. Walking into an office and showing up to a class without an idea of what you want to accomplish will not help you. A coach can only do so much, so take the time to sit down and write down your goals, even if it is just short term goals for now. Being sure of what you want shows the coach that you are dedicated and you are not wasting their time, resulting in a better relationship between you and the coach. Your coach should be someone you are comfortable with and with whom you can be honest about being tired or stressed as this will have an impact on your performance, and if they do not know these things they might push you harder than you think and you may end up having to sit out for a few weeks because of strain.

Being part of a group setting will also allow you to better your social skills, and even if you choose to do individual lessons, this will still force you to deal with someone else, in this case not letting you just stay in your room practicing in front of the mirror.

While I am advocating for getting a vocal coach I know that it is not always possible. If you absolutely cannot afford or find a vocal coach then it is also perfectly fine that you practice and learn on your own. I do however suggest that you find as many online and physical resources before jumping in head first.

Do your research on every single topic and know what you are doing before just trying an exercise, and running the risk of endangering your voice.

Common Policies

In this section I will cover the most common policies that most vocal coaches will have. While this is not something they absolutely have to have, it is important to know what the policies are for the coach you will be using. Each coach of course has their own rules and regulations when it comes to individual and group sessions as well as payments.

While these things are not set in stone it just lets you know that the coach is a professional and you will not run the risk of losing money or injuring yourself with someone who does not truly care about you or your voice.

There are various policies and regulations that I feel each coach needs. The following list is something I feel is extremely important. It is okay if not all of these are found out immediately but if some of these are missing and the coach cannot tell you why perhaps consider another option.

- Payment Policy
- Cancellation Policy
- Costs
- Location
- Accompaniment

These five things are some of the most important things to look for at first glance when you are shopping around for a vocal coach. I will cover different questions you might want to ask your vocal coach surrounding these five policies in the next section.

Payment policies are important as they will often let you know how the payment process looks for individual versus group sessions as well as the possibility of paying off the sessions or if you have to pay for multiple sessions in advance. This is especially important if you are looking for classes in a specific price range.

The cancellation policy that each coach has will differ from coach to coach. This might oftentimes also have an impact on your payment as most coaches will have a cancellation fee that has to be paid if the appointment is cancelled within a set period of time before the class. Most coaches also often have a policy that if the class is cancelled within a set period of time that you might be able to move the class or be refunded. Be sure to check these when looking at new coaches.

Costs are also important. No matter what you are willing to pay for a lesson, make sure that you are aware of all the payments that need to be made. Some coaches will have you pay a deposit of 50% before the class and then request the rest of the payment on the day of. Others will have payment structures setup, making it easier to pay off your classes or you might have to pay in advance, so be sure to check the initial costs and any other costs you might incur like traveling fees.

Location, location, location. This is one of the most important things to look out for. Some coaches will have their own studios, while others will have their lessons at their home. Be sure to check for the location of the classes as sometimes you might find out that the practice location is across town and this would change your financial situation as you might need to pay extra for traveling costs.

Accompaniment is an important thing to know. Some coaches will not use a piano to play along with singers while others might do this. If you are used to singing along to a piano, finding out if the coach can play piano or has someone play accompaniment is important as it might have an impact on the lesson costs.

All of these things are important to note, and can even be asked if there are no visible policies either at their studio, or on their website.

Questions

In this section I will cover a few basic questions that you should consider when looking for a vocal coach. Bursting in and bombarding a coach with a bunch of questions might leave them with a bitter taste in their mouth, so try and make the conversation as natural as possible. Like I mentioned before, this is going to be someone who you need to be open and honest with, and starting off bad might not be the best idea.

Do not be stuck with just one coach. Make sure that you do research, talk to people you know who are taking lessons, read up on coaches in your area, especially if you are looking for a coach for a specific genre and technique. Do not be trapped by just one coach.

The following questions are ones that you need to ask every single coach you will be seeing. It is important to note that if you ask any of these questions and the coach ignores it or refuses to give you a straight answer that something shady is going on and it might be a red flag, so be aware of that.

1. Education

When talking to your potential coach it is important to find out where they were taught, especially if you are getting coaching from a choir director. Most choir director degrees do not require that they learn how to teach someone to sing, instead only having to learn how to direct singers. It is extremely important that you know their basic educational background.

2. Experience

As with the above question, knowing how long they have done something will help you gauge how experienced they are. While a younger coach that has not been doing this for long is not necessarily a bad thing, an older coach isn't a bad thing either.

A younger coach might know some newer techniques and skills that they can teach you, or the older coach might know a little more overarching information on various genres instead of just being able to teach the basics.

3. Music Style

The music style for your coach is extremely important. While I understand that having one coach will be fine for the basics, it is important to note that if you are looking to go in a specific direction with your singing that it would be better to have a coach that can help you do that from the beginning, rather than having to change coaches after six months and having to change your entire routine because the second coach does things different.

When you first start out, search for coaches that can teach a variety of genres and if you meet a coach that may be able to help you, talk to them, discuss your goals, and go from there.

4. Accompaniment

As mentioned in the previous section about policies, it is important to know if you would need to arrange your own accompaniment player if it is needed, and if you would need to pay extra for that.

Most coaches spend their time teaching voice artists and do not necessarily play an instrument, so if you are used to singing with accompaniment then this is absolutely crucial.

5. Location

Oftentimes coaches will put up advertisements on campuses and notice boards in their area, but when you check their studio is across this city. So be sure to check where exactly their studio is and if they perhaps have a location closer to where you are living.

6. Costs and Policies

This is an important one and most coaches will have their price plans and policies up on their website, So make sure to check those out, and if there are any uncertainties do not be afraid to speak up and ask the coach about this.

I cannot stress this enough; it is extremely important for you to be comfortable with your coach. You will be spending a lot of time with them and if this is a career choice for you, doing something you love for hours on end with someone you do not like, or who does not like or respect you will slowly kill and drain the life from you. It is important that there is mutual respect between you and the coach, so when you ask your questions try and make it as natural a conversation that you can.

Do not feel pressured to pick a coach immediately. If you feel uncertain about a decision on which coach you want to pick then take the time to do some more research. Talk to them some more, communicate with them about your concerns and see if you and the coach can figure something out together.

Their final and only goal should be to have you feel comfortable, and if they are more worried about money than you and your wellbeing I would suggest looking for someone else. The difference between a good and bad vocal coach can be life changing, so be sure about the decision you make. While your decision might seem final, you can always move to another coach if you feel like the coach you are working with is not working out.

YOUR FIRST PROFESSIONAL LESSON

You have found a coach and you are happy with them. You are comfortable and you are about to go to your first lesson. In this section I will cover what to expect from your lesson and how to implement what you learned into practical knowledge that you can use to practice at home by yourself.

Before your Lesson

There are various things that you can do before your lesson to be prepared for your lesson. These things are basic , but they are important for a first lesson.

- Be sure to ask your vocal coach what you need to bring to the lesson. Often you will have to bring your own recorder to the session, but sometimes the coach may have their own recorder, which will make it far easier.
- Make sure to bring along a bottle of water for hydration.
- When you know that you will be in a location without a mirror, it is important to take your own. There is no need to bring a large mirror, a simple small mirror will be the perfect size.
- Always make sure you bring an extra copy of your sheet music. I suggest having two extra copies, especially if you are going to have accompaniment, so the piano player has their own copy of the song, making it easier for you to make notes without them having to worry about your notes.

During your Lesson

You have finally arrived at your first lesson, and it is going to be a thrilling experience. It is important to remember that during your lesson you will be learning new techniques. While this is happening it is important that your coach gives you notes and directions on how to improve or change your approach for it to be beneficial to you.

Constructive criticism is definitely something you should strive for, as having a coach who only praises you won't be teaching you anything. Criticism helps you grow and improve while praise won't do anything but make you feel good for a few minutes before moving on to the next section of the lesson.

One common practice that is important is the fact that your coach should suggest some practice exercises that you should try at home to put the things you learn to the test, so that the next time you have a lesson you have not forgotten what they had taught you. Be sure to follow these instructions and take notes on the exercises the coach gives you to do at home. Make sure you ask for more detail if you are struggling to understand a concept.

Most coaches will often use imagery to help you learn and improve your skills. They will explain how certain sounds will feel in your chest and throat and compare certain sounds to objects to help you better understand what they are trying to explain. This is common-place and can help you with your exercises at home.

After your Lesson

Now that you have finished your lesson it is time to put all the information and exercises into practice. It is important to remember to do the exercises your coach has given you, as it will help you improve.

It is important to remember that progress will be slow and major changes take between three and six months to be heard in your voice. Small changes will be noticeable after about a month, but patience is key.

It is important to practice at home, but remember to rest and not push yourself too hard. This will cause strain on your vocal cords and could set you back a week or two, delaying your entire improvement process. It is perfectly normal that you would want to focus on the small mistakes you and your coach found, but only focusing on those small mistakes will cause you to miss out on other important pieces of information and skills that you might need later on.

When creating your own routine to follow at home it is important to note that you need to create a balanced routine that includes enough rest and exercises so you won't become lazy or overwork yourself.

TOOLS TO GROW

Here I will be covering all the tools you might want to consider getting to be able to focus on your vocal training. Some of these tools are simple apps that you can use to keep track of your range, with the final part of this section covering different online coaches that can be followed on YouTube.

This section will be especially useful for those that cannot afford a coach or prefer to learn by themselves.

These resources will offer you all the guidance and help you may ever need, right at your fingertips.

Technology at Your Fingertips

The following section will cover a few apps that I have found to be quite promising and helpful when it comes to learning the new trade:

1. Swiftscales

Swiftscales simulates being able to sit at a piano and play while you are practicing. The app allows you to take the classes as fast or as slow as you need to, letting you take control of each and every single lesson.

What makes this app even more powerful is that your vocal coach can train with you via their cloud sharing settings.

2. 7 Minute Vocal Warm Up PRO

This app was developed by the world renowned vocal coach Indra Aziz, and offers you breathing exercises, warm up exercises, basic vocal exercises and even cool down exercises.

Indra has been a vocal coach for over 15 years and this app has been built to help you reach even greater potentials without having to struggle to find the appropriate warm up for your skill range.

3. Voice Training - Learn to Sing

This app offers you something that other apps do not. The capability to monitor your pitch and to help you correct it.

4. Yousician

Yousician is one of the industry standards when I think about apps that can help any level of singer. The app also offers classes for guitar, piano, ukulele and bass, making it easier to pick up an instrument as well.

Use the built in piano classes to learn the basics while also slowly and surely progressing through the classes and improving daily with the built in exercises and gameplay, creating a fun way to learn new skills.

5. Learn to Sing with Max&Maxine

Max and Maxine will guide you through their amazing app, offering you an entire singing course from start to finish.

The app offers you pitch control to help you adjust and control your pitch far better, as well as a way to record yourself during sessions, for later review or sharing.

6. Riyaz - Learn Singing - Vocal lessons and exercises

This app is truly one of a kind. The guided instructions help you live while you are recording and singing, making sure that you never miss that lost note or lost vocal again.

While the app is more targeted around Western and Indian classical musical stylings I would highly suggest trying out this app the next time you are looking for something a little more challenging.

7. Vocal Trainer - Learn to sing

Vocal trainer offers you a fun and educational way to get better at singing, very much like the rest of these apps this app will allow you to upskill.

What I love about this app is the fact that the vocal trainer aids you in understanding your vocal capabilities. It also helps you train note structure and logic far more intensely than other apps do.

The team that built this app created functionality that analyzes your recording information during a session and gives you feedback based on that analysis. Allowing you to find out which specific areas need training and then offering you training sessions for those specific areas.

8. Perfect Ear

The name says it all. This app offers you the unique capability of ear training. This is extremely important and while you can do so without an app, using the app will make the process easier to understand.

Perfect ear offers you the capacity to train even your solfège as well as note reading capabilities. The app also includes rhythm training and basic music theory, making this a perfect match for beginners and intermediates alike.

9. Complete Rhythm Trainer

This app will teach you the basics of rhythm, from reading to writing and rhythm identification, this app will teach you everything you need to know about rhythms.

This app was built similar to a video game, making the learning process fun while also educating you about the importance of rhythm in music and singing.

10. SingAlong

This app is a perfect companion for beginners that want to create their own sound, while also being able to enjoy the process.

The apps built in AI will analyse your karaoke sounds and suggest the best possible lyrics to go along your track selection, making your sound truly unique.

Blogs to Read

There are hundreds and hundreds of blogs online that share musical advice every single day. Many of them are singers, whilst others are vocal coaches or pianists or some are simply choir directors once a week on a Sunday.

In this small section I will share my top five blogs to follow if you want to stay in the know about music and the industry surrounding it while also continuously learning:

1. The Naked Vocalist
2. Open Mic UK
3. Ken Tamplin Vocal Academy
4. Felicia Ricci
5. School of Rock

Coaches to Follow

If you want to follow vocal coaches on YouTube and you wanna learn that way, then this section is specifically created for you.

I have found a few different coaches that have YouTube channels where you can spend hours upon hours watching their content to help you get better at belting or upskilling your singing or songwriting.

These are obviously not the only creators on YouTube that have these channels and create similar content but they are some of my favourites:

1. Madeleine Harvey

Madeleine covers topics that range from voice lessons, songwriting all the way to performance practices. She has a home style blog format on her channel and covers a more country genre selection of music.

2. Eric Arceneaux

Eric needs no introduction as he is currently one of the best and youngest vocal coaches in the industry. He has tons of knowledge and loves interacting with his audience. His New Orleans background makes him the perfect candidate for those looking at artists like Brett Manning.

3. Jacob's Vocal Academy

JVA hosts a myriad of vocal warm up techniques as well as training techniques that even beginners can follow. What makes this so amazing to me is the fact that this content is not only available on YouTube, but the guides can also be found on Spotify and Apple Music under the same name, making this a far easier content stream to follow or listen to while on the go.

4. Ron Anderson

Ron is one of the few creators and vocal coaches that follows the Voixtek method when it comes to coaching and teaching. His videos offer you in depth knowledge on how best to use your voice while also offer you a detailed guide and explanation of how exactly your voice works and how to produce certain sounds.

5. Freya Casey

Freya Casey is the resident opera singer and offers a wide variety of genre coaching and assistance on her channel. I love that she caters to the needs of the alternative community. She covers a wide variety of content from the best ways to keep your voice supple and how to keep your voice healthy and happy for a long career that will be sustainable.

MORE EXERCISES

In this chapter I will cover more exercises for both beginners and intermediate vocalists. These exercises can be used as warm up exercises, cool down exercises or as your main exercises during a rehearsal before putting those techniques into a song and testing your capabilities. Some of these exercises might test your endurance while others will push you to focus on vocal muscle building and maintenance. It is important to include different types of exercises as a way to make sure that your stamina stays strong and you will be able to perform no matter what the project or song may be.

Beginner Exercises

1. Vocal stress release method

This beginner vocal warm up exercise is one of my favorite exercises to suggest to anyone. It uses both physical movement and your vocal cords to warm up for your intense training session.

In this exercise you slowly stretch and massage various sections of your body while audibly inhaling and exhaling. To be able to do this simply stand with your feet shoulder width apart and inhale and exhale slowly.

Starting at your head, slowly tense and relax your body, muscle by muscle, slowly inhaling and exhaling, allowing all the stress and business of the day to melt away. Adding in movements like rolling your shoulders in small circles or having your fingers twitch and move around is perfectly fine. Remember to take your time, slowly moving down from your neck to your chest and torso and then your hips and legs.

Once you are done you can gently shake all the stiffness away from your body before moving on to the final part of the exercise. Like with normal muscles, if you gently massage and tense them for a little bit they will become more supple and will allow you to maintain the crips sounds you want to create. Simply continue to breathe deeply before gently massaging the sides of your neck, moving your left hand from your right shoulder all the way to the space below the right ear and doing the same on the left side. Once you have finished this you will move your hands to the front of your neck, or essentially your throat and gently massage the throat.

It is important to keep breathing deeply, not letting the air expand your chest but rather your torso and rib cage.

2. Lip bubbling

Lip bubbling is something I have noticed that quite a few beginners struggle with. This sounds extremely fun though and I absolutely love the sound this exercise creates.

To do this exercise, simply purse your lips and imagine that you are placing a straw in a glass and you are trying to create the sound it would make if you made the bubbles in the bottom of the glass. While this seems easy I know a lot of beginners struggle with this exercise as they use air to recreate the sound.

This exercise is completely independent of air. The main focus is to make a sound that's similar to bubbles popping. It may take you a few tries to figure out, and that is perfectly okay.

Just focus on trying to blow bubbles in the bottom of a glass without pushing air through your lips. The easiest way is to breathe through your nose for this exercise. It is also important to note to take small breaks in between the attempts that are tried with this exercise, one can quickly become light headed and that is not something we want to happen. If you are more advanced and your stamina and lung capacity is a little more than normal, be sure that you do not push yourself too far with this exercise.

3. Gargles

This is also one of my favorite exercises to give to beginners. It sounds simple and while it is simple to execute it may take some time to figure out.

To do this exercise remember to breathe. You will be gargling without having water in your mouth or throat. You will also be sliding up and down your range while doing this but if this is your first time attempting the exercise focus first on getting the technique right and then move on to the sliding part.

Sometimes it helps tilting your head back a little, I don't exactly know why but this seems to help some students. Take a deep breath and then slowly start to gargle. The sound will be very similar to the sounds that pigeons make when they are making the 'ooo' sound.

This is an excellent exercise to be able to relax the upper throat section. When you find that you can easily do this exercise you can move on to adding the sliding of your range to the exercise. Again, take your time, there is no rush, and forcing your voice and throat to make sounds you don't normally make will be strange and you might hurt yourself so be patient.

4. Vox training

This particular exercise was designed to train and improve your stamina. What is generally done is that the student will vocalize through a long tube. This tube will have the opposite end in water and the water that is bubbling because of the vocalization will create pressure to vocalize against and thus build stamina.

The Vox method is very easy to use but requires the Vox item from DoctorVox. The product allows you to warm up and exercise your vocal cords while also making sure not to dry out your throat.

5. Cardio

Most singers do not realize this, but cardio as a vocalist is extremely important and building up cardio and stamina will help you and your voice in the long run. To be able to build up cardio is one of the easiest exercises that you will come across.

To build up cardio, slap on some music and go for a jog. While you are jogging, find your favorite song and sing along. Now you do not have to belt out all the wonderful parts and put on an entire performance, but instead focus on your breathing and pitch while you are running. Doing this once or twice a week will help you slowly build up stamina and cardio, in turn giving you better breathing control and stamina.

6. Tiny singers

Tiny singers are similar to cardio singers, well at least in the singing part. This exercise also involves jogging, so if that has been something you have been wanting to do, now is the perfect time to do so.

Find your favorite song and go jogging, however instead of singing in a normal tone, you will focus on singing as softly as you possibly can. This is a rather difficult exercise as you will have to focus on volume control as well as air flow. Allow yourself just enough air to be barely audible. This might take a while to get perfect, but that is part of the exercise. You will not immediately be able to do this perfectly and that is fine, be sure to put in the time and effort into doing this.

Consider swapping between this and cardio singing when you are jogging, focusing one day on cardio singing and the next on tiny singing.

7. ISO exercises

Along with stamina building you will also have to build vocal muscle. It sounds silly but like with any other muscle in the body, the more you practice and use it the better it will be toned and the better it will work.

ISO or isolation exercises are a perfect trio of exercises that can be used to build vocal muscle. These exercises work hand-in-hand and though some may consider them to be scale exercises they are not. The ISO exercise is split into three exercises: falsetto slides, transcending tones and sirens.

These three activities isolate the muscle that is responsible for a certain sound and then strengthens that muscle by sliding through your range, in turn strengthens the muscles in an isometric fashion.

8. E screams

This specific exercise mainly focuses on the falsetto sound. The exercise is rather simple and anyone can do it. It just takes a little practice and getting used to it.

For this exercise you will choose one of the higher pitches in your vocal range and sustain that pitch at a very low volume, echoing a sound similar to an 'eee' in falsetto. Once you can comfortably sustain the pitch without faltering you can slowly push the pitch into a louder pitcher, letting the pitch become brighter and more cheerful.

This exercise and many like it create sounds that are very often found in horror movies, and even in rock and metal songs. So if that is a genre you are looking to get into this is the perfect exercise for you.

9. Minor scales training

This exercise, while for beginners can also be done by intermediate singers as it helps anyone that has not done this before. Most singers generally practice their scales in a major key, but in this exercise you will be practicing your vocal scales in a minor key.

To do this exercise, pick your favorite practice song and swap the key to a minor key. You can use the bubbles or gargle technique along with this to keep the exercise fresh and interesting. Now simply gargle the song in a minor key, giving it a new and refreshing twist.

10. 1000 challenge

This is the most fun exercise in my opinion, although this is a long one. For this exercise pick something like the gargle or bubbles, similar to how you did in the previous exercise.

Except this time instead of picking a song and changing the key signature you will be using your scales to do the lip bubbles exercise a 1000 times lover. This will not only help you get rid of nerves or anxiousness but this will entirely warm up your vocal cords for whatever is next.

I know 1000 seems daunting so start the project with 10, and if you can do those comfortably move on to 50, then 100, and then jump in intervals of 50 or 100's to finally end up being able to comfortably do 1000 lip bubble exercises. This exercise also helps when you are struggling to reach a certain pitch. To be able to practice your pitch, simply swap out the lip bubbles sound with the siren technique and you will soon come to realize that your pitch has changed and you can finally reach that note.

Intermediate Exercises

These exercises are generally created for singers and vocal artists with a little more knowledge and skill level, while you as beginner are more than welcome to try out any of these challenges as well. Similar to formatting in the beginner section I will cover some intermediate exercises for any type of day.

1. Speed Challenges

This exercise seems rather simple at first glance, but being able to support your voice during a speed run challenge is not something everyone can do.

To do this exercise choose a singular pitch that falls in the middle or lower parts of your vocal range, and sing the pitch on a 'hee' consonant/vowel sequence.

The sequence will be as follows: four times at a medium tempo and then eight times at a fast tempo, while sustaining the chosen pitch. Once you have successfully done this you can move the pitch up by half a step and then repeat the process until you are comfortable with moving between the steps.

2. Intervals of Fourths and Sixes

Fourth and sixth intervals are known for being tricky to spot and hear within different compositions, especially because they are used so often. In this exercise I will explain how to get comfortable with fourth and sixth intervals.

Before you can become comfortable with the previous mentioned intervals I would suggest starting this exercise by becoming comfortable with the third and fifth intervals.

The exercise can be split into three smaller exercises to get you comfortable with these two intervals. The first of the three encompasses the ability to break down a fourth interval, the second smaller exercise going from a third interval to a fourth interval, inherently testing your ear as well since there is only half a step between the two and third and final exercise incorporating a sixth interval sequence into the exercise that revolves down the third interval.

To start the exercise, pick a vowel and use a singular fourth interval in the lower vocal range to sing, repeat this for a few instances before moving on to the second exercise. Here you will go to a third interval, only half a step. Repeat this process until you are comfortable before moving on to the third exercise.

The third exercise will add in a sixth interval, adding in a full step between the chosen fourth step and the sixth step. Repeat the process until you feel comfortable and then start the entire process from scratch with a different vowel and low range fourth interval pitch.

3. Intervals of Octaves

As previously mentioned, an octave is the biggest interval that one can find. This exercise incorporates moving up an octave and down an octave until you are comfortable.

For this exercise select a pitch that falls into the lower ranges, opting for an 'a' vowel sound Once you feel comfortable doing this you can slide your pitch an octave up, and then end the exercise by sliding down an octave. Be sure to repeat the process over and over until you feel comfortable.

Once you feel comfortable doing so try eliminating the slide and then repeat the exercise in three distinct pitches.

4. Major Scaling

This is one of the most difficult exercises in the intermediate section and it is fine that you may struggle; that is what practice is for. Scales in general are a fantastic way to do some fine ear training. This exercise is difficult as it tests your capability of finding your highest and lowest pitch as well as your ability to move between these two pitches.

To do this exercise, you will find your lowest and highest pitch. Singing the lowest pitch first and then the highest, allowing your ears to register them will make this exercise a little easier to do.

Once you have done that start at the lowest pitch and sing the next note up. Think of this exercise as a staircase. Singing a note higher will mean taking one step up, and singing a note lower will mean taking a step down.

To complete this exercise, start with your lowest pitch and note by note step up until you reach a full octave, and then end the exercise by stepping down until you have reached an octave of steps again.

Advanced Exercises

While I did not cover advanced techniques throughout this guide, I do suggest moving on to these exercises if you feel comfortable enough doing the intermediate exercises and feel like you are no longer progressing.

You can also use a mix of beginner, intermediate and advanced exercises when you become comfortable enough, allowing you to slowly warm up your voice while making sure that all parts are covered and taken care of before jumping into a strenuous practice session.

The following exercises are generally used by advanced vocal artists.

1. Tongue Rolls

Tongue rolls, or more commonly known as the rolled r's technique, is a great way to make sure you have sufficient breath support and consistency during a song. Tongue rolls are important since even an advanced singer would need a full singer's breath to finish a rolled 'r' sound. If there is not enough air, the rolled 'r' sound will immediately stop once the air has dissipated.

This exercise is rather difficult so do not worry if you cannot do it the first few times that you try it. The goal here is to slowly progress and get better and better at it. To start this exercise find a comfortable vocal range for yourself, preferably in your vocal range and try the rolling r exercise on the single pitch. Once this is successful you can do the same thing on a pitch that is half a step lower. Continue doing this until your rolling r's are consistent and you do not cut off your sound.

Once you can create consistent rolling r's, you can move on to singing these rolling r's as a continuing phrase that will descend in a five note scale. You can choose to either go up or down. Continue this until it becomes a consistent scale.

2. Chromatic Scaling

Chromatic scaling is defined by the fact that the scales move up or down consistently, but only by a half step. An example of chromatic scale for C would be the following:

$$C - C\sharp - D - D\sharp - E$$

Chromatic scaling is rarely used in popular music and therefore much harder to finetune and stay in tune with them.

When you start the exercise, pick a vowel and start it with a five note chromatic scale and sing it in ascending order, in other words letting it step up half step. Once you can do this without hesitation of what the next note will be, you can move on to make it an eight note scale.

To end the exercise off, try and challenge yourself by doing a five note descending chromatic scale for fun.

3. Trumpet Vocalizations

This advanced exercise is derived from a warm up routine that is commonly used by trumpet players. This exercise is generally broken up in two sections and I highly suggest practicing each part until you feel comfortable with them separately before joining them together and then practicing it again until you feel comfortable.

The first part of the exercise is to sing each pitch for an eight note scale on the 'dee' in the middle vocal range, using only half steps to ascend the eight notes. It is important to remember that you only have to add the next half step note once you have completed the first 'dee' sound.

The second part of the exercise is to remove the 'd' consonant in the exercise and to replace it by singing the vocalizations as a legato vowel sound. Once again, only adding the half step once you have finished the previous legato vowel sound.

Try and keep a slow and steady pace when doing this exercise, nothing is rushing you. So take your time when you are working through this exercise to get it just right.

4. Trilling

trills are commonly more used in classical and traditional singing lessons, and almost every singer comes across them, somewhere in their learning stages or careers. They are not super difficult to learn, but they do take a while to get the hang of.

To start the exercise off, find a higher pitch that falls comfortably in your vocal range, be sure that you can comfortably sing this pitch for a short duration of time. Once you are comfortable with the pitch you have chosen you can move on to the next step. Now that you have chosen a starting pitch, sing the pitch one scale down from your starting pitch and then almost immediately switch back to the starting pitch.

Now that you know what both pitches are, switch between the two, gradually switching at a far more rapid pace. Once you feel comfortable with these two pitches, work through your entire vocal range, trying your best to get as comfortable as possible before switching to the next set of pitches.

All of these exercises will be helpful along your journey, and while you don't have to include all or any of them in your practice or warm up routine, I hope that these small practice exercises will help you improve your skill and expand your range and tone.

Related Chapters:

- Beginner
- Voice Health
- Vocal Range
- Music Theory
- Intermediate

OVERCOMING STAGE FRIGHT

In this chapter I will cover social anxiety and stage fright and how to overcome them so you can perform as smoothly as you practice.

Understanding Stage Fright

Being socially anxious is perfectly okay; everyone has some nervousness when it comes to being on stage for the first time, whether you are with a band or you are a soloist, or even when you are part of a choir.

Most of the time when you are anxious it is because your brain mistakenly believes that you are endangered. Your heart starts racing, you're shaking and every sound you hear feels ten times louder than normal. This is normal, as it is your body releasing adrenaline to allow you to get away as fast as you possibly can. Unfortunately, you are not actually in danger and this leaves you feeling breathless and dizzy.

It is perfectly normal to have stage fright, trust me, it happens to the best of us. One of the most common things that people do when they get stage fright is to keep it to themselves, and the feeling leaves you feeling rather isolated and like you are the only one experiencing it. If you have band members or choir members with you, speak to one of them, let them know that you are struggling to cope with the excitement of it all. More often than not, they will support and help distract you so you can forget about the nerves. If this does not help, or you are alone, try some of the following steps on how to deal with the high levels of excitement and anxiety.

Stage Fright Symptoms

Stage fright does not mean that you will not be able to perform or that you are inept at what you are doing.

The best way to counter stage fright is to figure out what caused it in the first place and then work towards fixing it.

Before we can work towards getting rid of your stage fright it is important to know how stage fright shows up. Not everyone experiences stage fright in the same way and more often than not people will only have one or two of the symptoms.

Some people deal better with stage fright and anxiety than others, so while you may show multiple of the symptoms we will be listing, you might feel calm enough to still go on stage while someone else will feel a single symptom and want to go home because the anxiety is too much for them.

It is important to remember that everyone is built differently and that not everyone deals with stress and anxiety in the same way. Some people tend to internalize while other people's stress and anxiety will be external. The best way to approach this is to be as open as possible when you notice that someone is struggling. Be as supportive as you can be. Some people might want a hug while others would just rather be left alone. Communicate with your choir members or band members and let them know that this is a safe space.

The following are common symptoms of stage fright:

- Racing heartbeat
- Narrowing and blurry vision
- Dry mouth, or cottonmouth
- Tightening of the throat
- Shaking and trembles, often one or the other but can be both
- Nausea
- Clammy hands and feet
- Feelings of cold extremities.

Stage Fright Causes

It is important to know what causes stage fright, especially if you want to counteract the stage fright in a healthy way.

Each person will be triggered by stage fright in a different way, and each person will experience stage fright for different reasons. Often you will find that certain people are more susceptible to stage fright and social anxiety than others, but remember that everyone can have social anxiety and it is perfectly okay to have it.

Realizing you have stage fright and knowing why you are having it will allow you to better understand and remedy the issues.

These are the five most common causes of stage fright:

1. Lack of Preparation

Not being prepared for what you are about to do is something that everyone suffers from, whether it is lack of preparation for an exam or not practicing a dance routine enough, there's always some sense of butterflies that make you feel unprepared for an activity.

The best way to counter and to fix this issue is to plan accordingly and make sure that you are constantly practicing and making sure that you are prepared for any type of situation within your control.

2. Lack of Experience

Like lack of preparation, lack of experience is something that happens when you feel that your knowledge and skill are not up to par. This often happens when people start a new hobby or activity and decide to compete or partake in group activities for the first time.

Luckily for you, and anyone else that is struggling with this, the easiest solution is to practice and study the subject matter as much as you can. If you come across an aspect you don't understand, ask a friend to explain it to you or do some more research on the topic.

If you happen to come across a skill you are not the best at, the best way to move forward and get away from inexperience is to practice and do the same thing over and over, allowing you to build up that experience.

3. Fear of Failure

No matter who you are or what your skill level is, the thought of standing in front of a large crowd and laying your soul out for all to see is terrifying and the fear of failing or making an idiot out of yourself is definitely something we all feel.

More often than not, the people who you think are sitting in the crowd, waiting for you to mess up and sing the wrong note or play the wrong riff, are also the people that will cheer the loudest for you if you succeed.

The best way to counter fear of failure is to focus on the positive side of things, try and avoid any negative commentary, and try to visualize the crowd cheering and clapping for you as you leave the stage. This will allow you to focus on the positive and thus lessen the fear of failure enough that you might even be able to forget about it completely.

4. Pre-existing Anxiety

Pre-existing anxiety is something some people just have. Some people are just born more anxious than others and more often than not end up in situations where their anxiety will only get the better of them.

If you are one of these people, don't worry. There are amazing methods for dealing with pre-existing anxiety, whether it is a medicinal remedy or a coping mechanism you have learned to deal with your normal anxiety, all will be well.

Simply use the same coping techniques and take a deep breath. It is only a bad second and not a bad life.

5. High Stakes

If you think about it, more often than not, the more pressure there is on a performance, for instance an entrance exam versus a class test, the more anxious you will be. The most important thing in these situations is to try and keep as calm as possible.

Keeping a positive attitude and visualizing a positive outcome will allow you to relax a little bit. Perhaps consider taking a few minutes to do a short breathing exercise to let your racing heart calm down and then focus on the task at hand. Worrying about things out of your control will only make your anxiety worse.

Take a step back from the situation and think to yourself "Can I control these circumstances?" If the answer is no, then move on to a situation where your direct input can have a direct impact on the outcome and focus positively on that instead.

The Day Before

1. Setting limits

Setting limits for yourself, whether it is to feel excited or nervous is extremely important. While it is normal to feel anxious and jittery, letting the feelings stew and stay for hours on end will only make the feelings stronger and more intense. Set a limit of perhaps an hour or two before moving on to other activities that will help peel your focus away from the anxious nerves you are feeling.

2. Visualization

Visualization is key. This is often difficult because it feels like you are trapped in a box and you cannot for the life of you find the exit. This is where focusing on the performance and the positive feelings it will bring will help you.

Close your eyes and take a few seconds to visualize and imagine how the performance will go. See the happiness that your performance brings people, and the excitement that it will bring you and the people you are playing and/or singing with. See the applause and the cheering at the end, that will bring you and your choir or band members happiness.

Visualizing something happy and cheerful will help you pull away from negative thoughts before and during the performance.

3. Endorphin exercises

Doing something that will release endorphins will also help you move away from the anxiety and dizziness you are feeling. You are always busy exercising, whether it is your dance routine, your voice or your instrument, so do not let the anxiety take that away from you.

Doing some physical exercise the day before and even on the day of the performance will release endorphins that will counteract the adrenaline rush you are getting and allow you to be calm and get a good night's rest. Be sure not to exhaust yourself as that may cause you restless sleep, leaving you tired and somber the next day.

4. Cat Videos

If everything else fails then you will have to resort to cat videos. Or at least to YouTube or Tik Tok for something funny to watch. Focusing on something that will make you laugh will pull your thoughts away from the negative and let you enjoy the last few hours before that important audition or stage performance.

Take the time to enjoy something on social media and focus on relaxation before the big day, nerves will only keep you from getting the rest you need.

The Day of Performance

1. Excess Adrenaline

When you are excited and pumped you are filled with adrenaline and the easiest way to get rid of it is to do some physical exercise. I suggest going for a jog the morning of the performance, or even a walk. If you are unable to do any of those things because you cannot go out, try and do some basic exercises at home before getting ready.

2. Breathe

Breathing is important when you are anxious and prone to stage fright. Take a few moments to close your eyes, center yourself and take some deep breaths. This will help you feel more calm and collected before you head onto the stage.

3. Caffeine

While caffeine is a replacement for water for most people, it should not be something you as a vocalist consume regularly. Caffeine in general is bad for your voice as it has a dehydrating effect on the vocal cords.

If you do drink a cup of coffee every so often, try and avoid it as much as possible on the day of the performance. The high levels of caffeine might spike your social anxiety even more and leave you feeling breathless and dizzy before you even get to the stage.

4. Smiles

During my high school years, I had a coach that would also tell me to smile, and then right after say "Fake it till you make it." This is one of the most important things to date for me.

Even if you do not feel like you are ready and excited for the performance, smiling is one of the most important things. Smiling can trick your brain into thinking that you are happy, releasing endorphins, and in turn leveling out the adrenaline for a potential anxiety attack or stage fright episode.

5. Confidence

The above mentioned advice can also be given here. False confidence is still confidence. Talk to the people around you about positive things, focus on the things you enjoy most about the set you are about to do on stage, especially focus on the things you do well.

This will leave you feeling confident, allowing you to walk onto stage with a good vibe, only letting the good vibes and feelings continue during your performance.

Practice Makes Perfect

One of the best ways to make sure that the stage fright stays away and the anxiety leaves you alone is to create a routine that you follow for each and every performance. This will trick your brain into thinking it is just another practice session instead of making you nervous because this is a "once in a lifetime" moment.

By doing the following things during your practice sessions you can easily fool your brain:

1. Practice daily

Make sure that you practice every single day.

If you are in a band and someone cannot join practice on certain days make the agreement that everyone will practice by themselves.

If you are a vocalist or in a choir, then make sure that you set a small time out every day to practice.

This will trick your brain into thinking that any performance is just a practice session and the stress of *needing* to do well will dissipate.

2. Positive statements

Before you practice, and after the practice session, take time with your choir or band members to say something positive about the session.

Whether you focus on yourself or the other members, saying something like "Your tone was fantastic today," or "Your singing was wonderfully harmonious," will bring positivity to you and leave no space for negative feelings to creep in.

This is also a perfect time to reassure yourself that you are doing great, and that all the hard work you have been putting into the practice sessions is paying off. Be kind to yourself.

3. Posture is important

Posture is one of the most important things when it comes to vocalists. Slouching over or not standing up straight closes off the larynx and chest, making it difficult to breath and produce the correct sounds.

Your brain is easily tricked into certain feelings. When standing up straight and with confidence your brain will believe that there is nothing wrong, thus avoiding the "there must be something wrong I need to flee" response that comes with anxiety and stage fright.

4. Meditation

Meditation is one of my favorite relaxation activities and I suggest taking it on to everyone. Even if it is just for five minutes before you go on stage.

To make this a habit, simply take five minutes of your time to cut yourself off from everyone and to sit down. Close your eyes and take your time to inhale and exhale, focusing only on good thoughts, especially things that make you happy and calm.

Once you have done this you can start your practice session. What makes this so fantastic is that it offers you calmness before going on stage as you will get to do this before you go on stage when you have a performance.

Meditate the Stress Away

As I have mentioned before, I believe that meditation is one of the most promising ways to help with stress relief and anxiety.

In this short section I will cover the importance of meditation for performing artists as well as some basic information to keep in mind when meditating.

There are various types of meditation that can be used by artists. The two most important and appropriate types I would suggest is guided meditation and mindfulness meditation.

Guided meditation generally goes hand in hand with an audio track describing scenery or a situation for you, allowing you to focus on those scenes. Guided meditation allows you to use as many senses as possible, allowing you to stay grounded and calm during the process. This will help keep anxiety from creeping up and making your stage fright worse.

Mindfulness meditation is generally for those more practiced in the art of meditation, and is based around acceptance of your surroundings and being aware of the present moment.

Both of these meditation methods will be helpful at different times. I suggest using mindful meditation during rehearsals. This allows you to focus on the practice at hand, without letting negative influences from the day impact your rehearsal and the rehearsal space.

On the other hand I would suggest using guided meditation during performance days. Finding a quick audio of ten minutes that will take you on a small journey, allowing you to focus on only the positive that will lie ahead in the performance.

Meditation has various elements that will help you manage and deal with your stress, whether it is the focused attention that drags your attention away from the anxiety, the relaxed breathing that will bring your heart rate down, the quiet setting that will further enhance calmness, and the comfortability and open attitude will allow you to fully immerse yourself into the mediation world, letting the worries melt away around you.

There are other ways to manage your anxiety and stress, and all those methods are valid. Be sure that you speak to a professional when you struggle to deal with small social interactions as there might be some bigger underlying issues. Be sure to talk with someone about any problems you might be having if it is impeding your social skills and any other mood or anxiety disorder that you might have.

I am not a medical professional and these opinions are purely based on experiences that I have had before.

CONCLUSION

In this full feature guide I hope that I have set your heart and anxiousness at ease when it comes to learning to sing. I hope that the resources I have shared will bring you as much joy as they have me.

When I sat down to write this guide, I knew I wanted to create a guide that contained all the basic information, but I did not want to bombard you with information that will make you feel like you delved in too deep. I tried to keep everything as basic as possible while also leaving you with enough resources to make the learning journey an interesting and passionate one.

I have always loved all forms of music, whether it is instrumentals or vocals. I have loved music since I was a small kid. It was a way of escaping any situation, even if it was just a boring commute back and forth from school or university.

Music, much like reading a book, creates an alternative universe where everything is possible and I hope that your journey with music and singing will be as blessed as mine was! The entire book, from the introduction chapter, all the way through to Chapter 4 of the intermediate section was a journey, and I felt exhilarated to be sharing this knowledge with you.

I hope and wish that the information I covered in this guide will help you become the singer you want to be, whether or not you want to be a vocal coach. I believe that everyone can sing, and that every single person that has the passion and will can be a beautiful singer, it just takes a little hard work and dedication.

I hope that you find your passion and love for music within these pages and that your wildest dreams can become a reality.

You have reached the end of your journey and you wish the utmost luck in all your future endeavors! May the knowledge you learned from this guide carry you through endless warm ups and vocal exercises, and even those terrible days before an audition when you are nothing but a nervous mess.

My last piece of advice will be this: do what makes you happy and confident. Do not let a vocal coach force you into anything you do not want to do and don't let people's opinions change your uniqueness!

GLOSSARY

Abduction: Opening one's vocal folds

Adduction: Closing one's vocal folds.

Arytenoid cartilage: Cartilage sections that are on the back of the cricoid cartilage. These sections are responsible for the vocal fold abduction and adduction.

Belting: A high impact sound, generally used within contemporary music genres, that can be compared to shouting. These sounds are generally used to create emotionally charged sounds within a track or song.

Breathiness: The sound of breathing in songs or tracks when air escapes via the glottis. This generally occurs when the larynx is not sufficiently trained or there is inefficient vocal fold closing.

Cambiata: Male voices during the adolescent phase and the changes that go along with adolescence. This is especially used when the changed vocal pitch range is not classified as an alton, baritone, bass or tenor pitch.

Contemporary Commercial Music (CCM): Music genre that includes subgenres of musical theatre, pop and rock, gospel, folk and any other musical vernacular that is similar in sound.

Creak: Irregular vocal fold sounds that create a sound at the lowest possible pitch.

Cricoid cartilage: Circular, ring-shaped cartilage that forms part of the lower section of the larynx.

Cricothyroid: Muscles that contract and pull the thyroid down to create a higher pitched sound by creating vibrations in the vocal folds.

Cross-training: This is generally used to describe an array of training methods for voice or musical artists.

Deep neck flexors: These muscles are tasked with keeping the cervical vertebrae straight during training and singing.

Diaphragm: A dome-shaped muscle that helps with pulling air into the lungs during the breathing process when you sing or do breathing exercises.

Dysphonia: Generally considered to be any vocal or voice function problems or disorders. Typically found when voice artists push themselves too hard, don't exercise their vocal cords correctly or get sick and strain the vocal cords.

Epiglottis: A section of cartilage that closes over the top of the larynx when you swallow to keep food or liquid from entering your larynx. This helps with choking and air intake.

Expiration: Commonly known as breathing out. The opposite of Inspiration, seen later in the glossary.

Falsetto: A sound that creates a higher vocal range, common in women and children, also called Head Voice for women and children.

Formant: relatively strong group of harmonics. A formant can be reinforced in a resonant cavity or space with the corresponding resonant frequency. There five formants. In the voice, the first two formants define the vowel quality. Formants three, four and five define other aspects of vocal quality, mostly concerned with the projection of the voice.

Frequency: The number of vibrations per second in the sound.

Fundamental Frequency: The lowest and most powerful frequency that can be found in a range.

Glottis: Spaces that can be found within the vocal folds.

Harmonics: Vibrations within a harmonic group. Harmonics can be found in the entire sound spectrum range.

Laryngeal constriction: The action of closing your larynx. This will cause a crass sound that is not generally used within music.

Larynx: The organ that contains the vocal folds. The larynx is primarily used to stop air from filtering into the lungs while also having a secondary function to keep air inside the lungs for when it is needed and a third function that allows you to be able to create sound.

Loudness: The amplitude and volume of a sound that has been created. It is usually measured in decibels (dB).

Motor memory: A rehearsed muscle spasm that is encoded in the brain as a normal regular pathway.

Mucosal layer: A moist mucous layer on the outside layers of the vocal folds that keep the vocal folds healthy and safe.

Onset: The first part that can be heard from any sound.

Glottal: Sounds that normally start with a click, similar to sounds that are used for exclamations. These sounds are created when the vocal folds are pressed together and before you exhale.

Aspirate: Sounds that can be found when air escapes the vocal folds, these sounds are also audible sounds that happen before tone begins.

Creak: Sounds that are created to sound like creaking doors or windows and are often created by vibrating the vocal folds.

Pharyngeal constrictor: The muscles that surround the larynx. When constricted they push the larynx up, creating the swallowing mechanism.

Pharynx: The section found between the larynx and the large opening at the back of the mouth, more commonly known as the throat.

Pitch: Both the complex sound waves and frequencies that are created by a sound. Upper harmonics will allow us to hear more tonal color when hearing the fundamental frequencies.

Posterior glottis chink: This small gap can be found behind the back of the vocal folds when one is talking. It is commonly found with poor muscle control surrounding the arytenoid cartilages. This is most commonly found in women and creates a breathy tone of voice.

Puberphonia: When one uses a falsetto voice to speak, b0th during and after puberty. This is usually found in those who are reluctant to accept the change their voice is going through.

Repertoire: The music a single artist knows, generally their own songs, sometimes single tracks or often choral music.

Roughness: This sound is created by irregular vibrations within the vocal folds and creates a grating sound.

Soft palate or velum: The soft tissue at the back of the roof of the mouth. When raised, it forms a seal between the mouth and the nasal cavity. During swallowing, this action prevents food from entering the nose.

Strap muscles: The muscles that are used to lower the larynx.

Support: The action of maintaining your breathing for singing purposes.

Thyroarytenoid: A muscle within the vocal fold that helps control vocal fold vibration when contracted, lowering the frequency.

Tongue retraction: When you are pulling your tongue back into your mouth, causing vowel distortion.

Tongue root tension: Pressing the base of the tongue against the hyoid bone. Can also be felt when putting pressure underneath the chin.

Vibrato: Fluctuation in loudness that is generally considered to be a periodic action that lasts in seven second cycles. This may be caused by tremors or a natural phenomenon.

Vocal folds: Tissue that is stretched across the larynx in the horizontal fashion. They help with valve functionality for the larynx. When the vocal folds are brought together the edges can vibrate and make a sound.

Vocal health: Your vocal fold health and vocal system health, but more specifically the health of your vocal folds.

Vocal ligament: The length within the membrane of the vocal folds, and contribution to strength of the vocal folds. Rarely seen in infants and can be seen more in teen and adolescents vocal folds.

Vocal loading: A sense of strain that can be found on the voice, usually found with excessive voice usage, excessive volume and loudness and higher anxiety levels.

Vocal register: The human voice range. This can be defined as the vibrations that happen within the vocal folds. When there are lower registers the vocal folds will vibrate where the mucous cover over the vocal folds will vibrate in higher registers.

Vocal tract: A space found between lips or nostrils and the vocal folds. Consists of the epilarynx, pharynx, oral as well as nasal cavity.

Vocalis: Muscles found along with the vocal folds as well as the thyroarytenoid. Vocalis is attached to the front of the thyroid cartilage and the back of the arytenoid cartilages. Contraction of the vocalis makes the vocal folds shorter and lowers the frequency, in turn also lowering the vocal fold vibration.

Vowel modification: Making the choice to consciously alter vowels to create exploitation of the resonant properties of vocal tracts at specific pitches.

Dear reader,

Thank you for reading *The Do-Re-Mi of Singing*.

If you enjoyed this book, please leave a review where you bought it. It helps more than most people think.

Don't forget your FREE book chapters!

You will also be among the first to know of FREE review copies, discount offers, bonus content, and more.

Go to:

https://offers.SFNonfictionBooks.com/Free-Chapters

Thanks again for your support.

REFERENCES

B, A. (2021). *Best Singing Resources for 2020*. Tutorful.co.uk. https://tutorful.co.uk/blog/best-singing-resources-for-2020-1

Icon Collective. (2018, October 24). *Basic Music Theory for Beginners - The Complete Guide | Icon Collective*. Icon Collective College of Music. https://iconcollective.edu/basic-music-theory/

L, M. (2014, June 10). *Teach Yourself How to Sing: 5 Helpful Tools*. Take-Lessons Blog. https://takelessons.com/blog/teach-yourself-how-to-sing-tools

Mayo Clinic. (2020, April 22). *A Beginner's Guide to Meditation*. Mayo Clinic. https://www.mayoclinic.org/tests-procedures/meditation/in-depth/meditation/art-20045858

McQuerrey, L. (2019, January 29). *Where to Start When You Want to Be a Singer?* Work - Chron.com. https://work.chron.com/start-want-singer-25776.html

Music Genre Admins. (2009). *Music Genres List*. Music Genres List. https://www.musicgenreslist.com/

Music Theory Team. (2019). *musictheory.net*. Musictheory.net. https://www.musictheory.net/

Musika. (2016, October 28). *Vocal Exercises: Intermediate and Advanced*. Musika Lessons Blog. https://www.musikalessons.com/blog/2016/10/vocal-exercises-2/

Oren, L. (2020, March 26). *Online singing lessons: the pros and cons*. Singwell. https://singwell.eu/online-singing-lessons/

School of Rock. (2018a, May 10). *School of Rock | 7 Tips to Keep Your Singing Voice Healthy*. School of Rock. https://www.schoolofrock.com/resources/vocals/7-tips-on-how-to-keep-your-singing-voice-healthy

School of Rock. (2018b, May 23). *School of Rock | How to Overcome Stage Fright.* School of Rock. https://www.schoolofrock.com/resources/music-industry/how-to-overcome-stage-fright

School of Rock. (2019a, February 28). *School of Rock | Private Music Lessons Versus Group Music Lessons.* School of Rock. https://www.schoolofrock.com/resources/music-education/which-is-better-private-music-lessons-versus-group-music-lessons

School of Rock. (2019b, May 31). *9 Best Vocal Warm-Ups for Singers | School of Rock.* School of Rock. https://www.schoolofrock.com/resources/vocals/9-best-vocal-warm-ups-for-singers

School of Rock. (2021, October 18). *How to Find Your Vocal Range.* School of Rock. https://www.schoolofrock.com/resources/vocals/how-to-find-your-vocal-range

SuperiorSinging. (2018, January 4). *How To Sing For Beginners - 3 Tips for Fast Vocal Improvement.* Www.youtube.com. https://www.youtube.com/watch?v=oIYDK1Jsr14

Turk, K. (2019). Church Hymn I am Resolved. New Years Resolutions! [Camera]. In *Unsplash.com.* Kiy Turk on Unsplash">Photo by Kiy Turk on Unsplash

Tymmi. (2020, July 23). *How to Choose An Apt Music Genre.* The Young Musician Music Institute. https://www.tymmi.com/music-genres-how-to-choose-appropriate-one/

Vendera, J. (2021, February 16). *10 Best Vocal Exercises for Singers | Sweetwater.* InSync. https://www.sweetwater.com/insync/best-vocal-exercises-for-singers/

Western Michigan University. (n.d.). *GLOSSARY OF MUSICAL TERMS* (pp. 1–12). Retrieved October 29, 2021, from https://wmich.edu/mus-gened/mus150/Glossary.pdf

Williams, J. (n.d.). *Glossary of Singing Voice Terminology.* Retrieved October 29, 2021, from https://www.jenevorawilliams.com/wp-content/uploads/2017/12/Book-glossary.pdf

AUTHOR RECOMMENDATIONS

Play in Perfect Harmony

Discover how to express yourself through rhythm and notes, because music theory doesn't have to be intimidating or tedious.

Get it now.

Teach Yourself to Meditate

Discover your inner peace, because this book has 160+ meditations to choose from.

Get it now.

www.SFNonfictionBooks.com/Meditation-Workbook

ABOUT AVENTURAS

Aventuras has three passions: travel, writing, and self-improvement. She is also blessed (or cursed) with an insatiable thirst for general knowledge.

Combining these things, Miss Viaje spends her time exploring the world and learning. She takes what she discovers and shares it through her books.

www.SFNonfictionBooks.com

amazon.com/author/aventuras

goodreads.com/AventurasDeViaje

facebook.com/AuthorAventuras

instagram.com/AuthorAventuras

Printed in Great Britain
by Amazon

33300352R00076